Wally Seccombe
D. W. Livingstone

"DOWN TO EARTH PEOPLE"

beyond class reductionism and postmodernism

Garamond Press

Printed and bound in Canada

Garamond Press,
63 Mahogany Court,
Aurora, Ontario
L4G 6M8

Cover Illustration: Hamilton Action Days march, February 1996

Canadian Cataloguing in Publication Data

Seccombe, Wally, 1945-
"Down to earth people" : beyond class reductionism and postmodernism

Includes bibliographical references and index.
ISBN 1-55193-019-6

1. Iron and steel workers - Ontario - Hamilton - Attitudes. 2. Working class -Ontario -Hamilton - Case studies. 3. Class consciousness - Ontario - Hamilton - Case studies.
1. Livingstone, D. W., 1943- . II. Title.

HD8039.I52C38 2000 305.5'62'0971352 C99-932432-2

"DOWN TO EARTH PEOPLE"

Contents

Acknowledgements

This book is one of the results of more than a decade of collaborative research on two related studies - the Steelworker Families Project and the Hamilton Families Project - both supported by research grants from the Social Sciences and Humanities Research Council of Canada. Our deepest gratitude goes to our co-investigators, June Corman and Meg Luxton, for their countless contributions and persistent commitment to completing the general project in spite of many obstacles.

This short volume is a reworked extension of the final chapter of *Recast Dreams: Class and Gender Consciousness in Steeltown* (Toronto: Garamond Press, 1996). That book deals with the general context of contemporary class and gender relations, current conceptions of class structure and class and gender consciousness, and empirical assessments of these conceptions using our Hamilton interview data. There are two other related books: *Recasting Steel Labour* by June Corman, Meg Luxton, D.W. Livingstone, and Wally Seccombe, (Halifax: Fernwood Publishing, 1993), which deals with restructuring in the steel industry; and *Getting by in Hard Times: Gender and Class Relations in Steeltown* by Meg Luxton and June Corman (Toronto: University of Toronto Press, forthcoming), which addresses the coping patterns of daily life.

Many members of United Steelworkers Local 1005 at Stelco's Hilton Works and their spouses, as well as many other Hamilton residents, willingly participated in our surveys, in-depth interviews, and numerous other discussions, providing an exceptionally rich information base. The sample surveys were administered by Social Data Research of McMaster University and the Institute for Social Research at York University. Marshall Mangan conducted much of the quantitative data analysis and co-edited *Recast Dreams*. Laszlo Gyongyossy, Esther Reiter, and Rhona Shaw assisted in the initial round of in-depth interviews. Elizabeth Asner conducted the first round of supplementary in-depth interviews. The most recent follow-up interviews were conducted by Belinda Leach, who has continued to extend this data base in her own research. Important technical and research assistance was also provided by Andrew Clement, Doug Hart, Niamh Hennessey, Matt Sanger, and other graduate research assistants at OISE/UT.

Text processing has been assisted by Jill Given-King and Kristine Pearson, and the copy editing for this volume by Ted Richmond. A special thanks to Garamond Press publisher Peter Saunders for prodding us to revise the original chapter as a book and then hustling it through to completion.

Author Profiles

D.W. Livingstone is a professor in the Department of Sociology and Equity Studies in Education at the Ontario Institute for Studies in Education of the University of Toronto. His related publications include: *Class, Ideologies and Educational Futures* (Falmer Press, 1983); *Working People in Hard Times* (Garamond Press, 1987); *Recast Dreams: Class and Gender Consciousness in Steeltown* (Garamond Press, 1996); *Public Attitudes Toward Education in Ontario 1998: The Twelfth OISE/UT Survey* (University of Toronto Press, 1999); and *The Education-Jobs Gap: Underemployment or Economic Democracy* (Westview Press and Garamond Press, 1999).

Wally Seccombe is an associated instructor in the Department of Sociology and Equity Studies in Education at OISE, University of Toronto. His related publications include: *A Millenium of Family Change: Family Forms and Modes of Production* (Verso, 1992) and *Weathering the Storm: Working-Class Families from the Industrial Revolution to the Fertility Decline* (Verso, 1993), and 'Contradictions of Shareholder Capitalism: Downsizing Jobs, Enlisting Savings, Destabilizing Families' in *Socialist Register* (Merlin Press, 1999).

Introduction

Workers are not stupid. They seem to think that if you're in a factory or whatever that you're stupid, that you don't have a brain.

-Donna, Hamilton working-class woman, 1994.

The class analysis of capitalist societies has come under withering fire in recent times. The critique of marxism's "class reductionism"viewing the world too simplistically through a class lens - is well taken. Yet many social theorists, including former marxists, seem quite prepared to bid adieu to the working-class and class struggle in "post-industrial societies."[1] In celebrating the previously silenced voices of women and people of colour, they have become increasingly oblivious to class cleavages in comprehending the dynamics of modern societies. Instead of integrating other core divisions with a class analysis to create a more comprehensive framework for understanding the reproduction of inequality in contemporary societies, many progressive theorists - particularly in the postmodernist genre - have stood the original marxist error on its head, treating class dynamics as an afterthought. That is what marxism had done with gender, what Western feminism had done with race, what pan-African studies had done with ethnicity. Is it really necessary to repeat this error again, coming full-circle in an endless reiteration of essentialist categories?

As the working-class voices from Hamilton cited in this study will demonstrate, the death of class has - in Mark Twain's words - been "greatly exaggerated." But we are not claiming that nothing much has changed. There have been subtle yet far-reaching mutations in working-class consciousness in the past two decades as the discipline of the labour market has intensified and the rise of neo-liberalism has made wage-earning families feel more vulnerable and insecure. These pressures have resulted in declining support for affirmative action programs for women and minorities and welfare assistance to the poor. These changes will be explored at some length below.

This book proposes a substantial revision of the orthodox marxist approach to understanding group consciousness and action. The tendency to anchor all forms of collective struggle and consciousness in prevailing relations of production is now conceded by both scholars and political activists to be inadequate. The social movements of oppressed peoples that have swept the globe during the post-WWII era—movements for national self-determination, the civil rights of visible minorities and the liberation of women—have conclusively demonstrated the deficiencies of this viewpoint. We seek to break with a "class first" framework which treats gender, generational, and race relations as subsidiary to, or somehow derived from, class relations. But unlike so many scholars who have made their break with marxist orthodoxy by embracing some version of postmodernist discourse theory, we remain steadfast materialists.[2]

The relentless skepticism of the postmodernists has usefully subverted established dogmas and opened a critical space for rethinking issues of group identity. Fortunately, we are not forced to choose between a deconstructionist ascent into the rarefied atmosphere of linguistic idealism or a retreat into the well-worn ruts of marxist fundamentalism. Progressive social theorists now need to mount a vigorous effort of *reconstruction*, weaving together strands of a provisional alternative. In this volume, we explore the outlines of a revised marxist approach, based upon three interrelated concepts:

- a multilateral conception of social interest;
- a culturally immersed understanding of group identity;
- an episodic account of people's propensity to engage in collective struggle that relies more upon their sense of the

> prospects for success, fluctuating as the situation changes, than on the cumulative impact of deprivation and grievance which lays the emotional groundwork for rebellion.

To ground our own rethinking on these issues, to keep us "down to earth," we listened closely to Hamilton steelworkers and their spouses who offered us their analysis of the world today and their thoughts on its multidimensional inequalities. Two couples in particular from our many informants - one older and one younger - have been chosen as representative of their generation. (See the Appendix for a description of the Hamilton population we sampled and the sample's composition). As the book progresses, we shall share with you a generous sampling of their reflections which inform our analysis at every stage. Since we are striving to rework the marxist paradigm by revisiting the terrain of its greatest strength, the relation between class structure and working-class consciousness is central to the discussion.

Hamilton Steelworkers and their Spouses:

Unsettling the Core of the English-Canadian Working-Class

Working people are living through a period of rapid change in patterns of work, paid and unpaid; this is inducing a reorientation of life-choices and family coping-strategies. The overarching process reshaping the world today has been dubbed "globalization" or "global restructuring." Globalization is not new; the spread of market economies around the world got underway in the era of mercantile capitalism four centuries ago. Restructuring has been a continuous feature of capitalist development ever since, marked by headlong technological change, the unplanned fluctuations of the business cycle, and waves of competitive destruction - thriving firms driving their inefficient rivals out of business. Periods of economic stagnation and crisis followed by periods of re-settled employer-employee relations, resumed economic growth and relative social stability, have been endemic to capitalism since its inceptrion, (see Maddison, 1982).

The upside of 'market freedoms' for working people is that they are legally free to quit work, move around the country, and compete for any job available in the national labour market. The downside is insecurity in the basic conditions of life. While social conservatives are inclined to blame the family's ills on sexual permissiveness, moral degeneracy and creeping welfare-socialism, the truth is that unregulated capitalism is hard on families, even small, mobile, nuclear families. In shortening most forms of commercial contract, the free market militates against the long-term obligations to one's partner, parents and children that enable families - in whatever form - to provide reliable support, binding three generations together over the life-course. In eroding the subsistence-base of the economy and commodifying every consumable, unfettered capitalism draws people into the paid labour force and devalues the unpaid work done at home, overwhelmingly women's work, that provides for such elementary family pleasures as sitting down and eating a home-cooked meal together. The more atomized, turbulent and rootless economies become, the more difficult it is to justify costly childbearing, long-term monogamy, or taking time off paid work to care for one's elderly parents.

For most working-class families, the post-war boom from the 1940s to the mid 1970s offered a respite from this unsettled existence. For three decades, job-creation was strong, unemployment remained low, and the basic provisions of the Welfare State were consolidated, substantially alleviating the vulnerability of workers and their families to layoffs, sickness and work-related injuries. But when this extraordinary boom petered out in the recession of 1973-75, the basic conditions of working-class insecurity began to reappear. While economic growth slowed, the pace of technological change quickened. The integration of the world economy took a quantum leap forward as investment capital began to zip around the world in volumes that dwarfed the currency reserves of the world's central banks. As the cost of moving money, information and goods fell sharply, local economies became increasingly specialized and vulnerable to forces beyond their control. Investors could pull the plug on countries whose business climate looked troubling, and companies found it easier to close plants and move to regions where labour costs and tax rates were lower and environmental regulations weaker.

Politically, neo-liberalism became ascendant, led by parties of the Right; the major parties of the Centre and Left reluctantly followed suit.[3] The champions of *laissez-faire* urged governments to make labour markets more flexible. This would be a blessing for working families if it meant that employees had more discretion in determining their conditions of employment. But rather than flexibility *for* workers, more often it is a case of the obligatory flexibility *of* workers, bending to employers demands in order to keep their jobs. What neo-liberals really mean by labour flexibility is that it ought to be easier *for employers* to:

- lay-off workers at any time;
- replace permanent staff with part-time workers who do not qualify for benefits;
- contract out corporate functions to specialized firms who hire unorganized workers on short-term contracts and pay them less;
- schedule more overtime to avoid recalling laid-off workers or hiring new ones; and
- transfer production to regions with lower labour costs and fewer employment regulations.

When companies are free to treat workers as dispensable commodities, they make the labour market *less* flexible for their employees. Household routines are disturbed by changes in the way firms contract with labour and schedule shifts.[4] Just-in-time production schedules are organized to fill customer orders, tighten inventory levels, and secure technological efficiencies in batch processing. Staffing plans must be finalized later - just in time - and workers are provided with less advance notice of their shift-schedules. In consequence, family events become harder to plan. Intensified competition in consumer markets fosters extended selling hours. As stores stay open later and Sunday shopping proliferates, retail employees must work more evening and weekend shifts. In Canada, nine-to-five days and the five-and-two week comprise a shrinking proportion of all employment schedules. In 1976, 65% of Canadian workers put in a standard work-week; by 1995, only 54% did.[5]

The deregulation of the working week has complicated family time-management, exacerbating the trade-off between making money and "making time" (Schor, 1992; Hewitt, 1993). The more hours the members of a household need to devote to paid work, the harder it is to set aside family-time together. When the work schedules of two or more members of the household cannot be synchronized, family meals together during the week are rare and sleep-times are disparate. The unpaid domestic work that directly sustains family life is thus forced to adapt to the pre-determined timetables of work and school.

Since women still do the great bulk of family-care work, even when they work outside the home, it falls to them, much more than to men, to reassemble what the demands of the external world have pulled apart - making-do with disjointed meal-times, feeding the kids while preparing to eat later with one's husband, caring for people coming and going at odd hours. As it becomes much more difficult to co-ordinate the family's life together, time-management issues become a major bone of contention between spouses.

Changes in the labour market have shaken up the life-course as well. As the pace of technological change accelerates, occupational skills become outmoded more quickly and career employment paths are more difficult to sustain; promotional ladders are disrupted by corporate downsizing, mergers, takeovers and plant closures. As middle-aged workers who have worked for the same company for years lose their jobs, employers and politicians propose retraining and life-long learning as antidotes to a growing sense of insecurity. Young people in their late teens and early twenties find it increasingly difficult to enter the full-time labour force and become self-supporting adults. Between 1990 and 1995, the average income of Canadians aged 15 to 24 fell 20%.[6] High levels of youth unemployment have forced many young adults to return to school and live with their parents far longer than either generation would have wished. The whole process of "growing up and settling down," obtaining a job with real prospects, finding a mate, living together, getting married and having kids, is delayed, disrupted, rendered uncertain and reversible.

Underlying all these trends was the prolonged economic slowdown from the mid 1970s to the early 90s. It meant that most firms could grow only by bringing new products to market, cutting prices and taking market-share from their competitors. As competitive pressures intensified, companies were compelled, under penalty of slow death, to shorten production cycles and lower per unit costs by replacing older plants and inefficient technologies. They did so in two ways:

- by renovating existing facilities, replacing outmoded machinery with newer technologies, reorganizing production and downsizing existing work forces; and

• by shutting down old plants or leaving them to wither and die while setting up new, state-of-the-art facilities at "greenfield" sites.

In the steel industry, both forms of capital renewal have occurred. The mushrooming of mini-mills in the past two decades is a textbook case of the latter route, capital circumvention. Most mini-mills were built by new companies who placed them in rural districts within easy reach of major cities, brought in outside management teams and recruited inexperienced production workers from the local area, by-passing the sector's established unions.

Cheap steel from the upstart mini-mills put tremendous pressure on the long-established steel companies to raise productive efficiency, cut costs and adapt their product-line to better meet market demands. Feeling the competitive heat, Stelco (the Steel Company of Canada) scrambled to renovate Hilton Works, its flagship plant in Hamilton, introducing continuous casting and slashing its work force by more than half from 1981 to 1992. As well as disrupting the lives of those who lost their jobs permanently, these changes have altered irrevocably the lives of Hilton's remaining steelworkers and their families.

During the post-World War II period of economic expansion, many unionized male workers in heavy industry had secure well-paying jobs and came to think of themselves as middle-class - hard-working, reasonably comfortable, certainly not poor or lower-class. Their identities as men were based upon being reliable family breadwinners. With very few jobs available to married women, the demand that employed men be paid "a living wage" (sufficient to support a family of four in relative comfort) became a cornerstone of labour's righteousness (Seccombe, 1993). Workers said to their employers, in effect: "if we were decently paid, our families could live decently without having to beg or borrow from anyone. Our wives could remain at home and become good homemakers, just like your wives; and our children could stay at school and get a good education, just like your children." By the values the propertied classes held dear, these were wholly honourable goals; they were nevertheless jeopardized by the employers' demand for cheap labour. In highlighting the discrepancy, unions put employers on the defensive and condemned the operation of the free labour market by the criterion of a higher value - the sanctity of the family - venerated by "respectable" members of all social classes. The notion that men ought to be their families' sole income-earners while women remained at home caring for their husbands and children was not only a prevailing cultural ideal; in Hamilton during the postwar boom, it became the predominant form of the domestic economy for the great majority of working-class families.

Our research with steelworkers at Hilton Works began in the early 1980's as this entrenched pattern of work-and-family relations was unraveling. In 1980, local 1005 of the United Steelworkers of America was the largest union local in the country with 13,025 members. But Stelco's markets were threatened by gluts of cheap imported steel, and management pushed for major concessions in preliminary contract talks with the union. The local's leadership refused to bite and a strike became inevitable. It lasted an agonizing 125 days. The timing of the 1981 strike was extremely unfortunate both for the company and the workers - but especially for the latter. As the strike dragged on, many of Stelco's customers went elsewhere and the settlement was immediately followed by the beginning of an extensive plant restructuring and a protracted series of layoffs as labour-saving technologies were introduced. By 1983, the 1005 membership had plummeted to 7,975. Customary family subsistence strategies were disrupted, even for those who managed to keep their jobs. Many suffered repeated layoffs and years of uncertainty not knowing whether they would be later be recalled.

Table 1: Stelco's Hilton Works Hourly Employees, 1980-1996

Year	1005 Bargaining Unit
1980	13,205
1981	12,576
1982	11,196
1983	7,975
1984	9,731
1985	9,972
1986	8,556
1987	8,129
1988	7,850
1989	7,390
1990	7,291
1991	6,607
1992	5,690
1993	5,170
1994	5,463
1995	5,317
1996	5,195

Source: Stelco Hilton Works Personnel Reports, October 1989 and November 1996.

The "fear of falling" became palpable among 1005 members and their families.[7] Many men spoke of not being able to sleep at night, worried sick about losing their jobs. For middle-aged steelworkers, there is a rational basis to this apprehension. They have less education than most people who earn equivalent incomes and their skills are often quite specific to steelmaking and not readily transferred to other fields of employment. Traditionally, the main attraction of working for Stelco was that "the work is steady and the pay is decent." Now the first half of that equation was gone. They'd worked hard all their adult lives to make a home and raise a family, paying down the mortgage and putting their kids through college or university (where very few went themselves). They were proud of being dependable breadwinners who earned their families keep, paid their taxes, were law-abiding citizens and members-in-good-standing of the local community. They'd fought for stability against the vagaries of an unstable system. Now that stability was threatened.

Their fierce devotion to staving off insecurity is often accompanied by fear and resentment of the poor, who appear, from their vantage point, to lead dissolute, disordered, lives, dependent upon the state for handouts. The message of neo-liberal parties vowing to cut income taxes while reducing welfare payments often finds a receptive audience among the upper layers of the industrial working-class, as a close examination of voting patterns for the Harris-led Tories in the past two Ontario elections will demonstrate.[8]

With the earning capacity of Hamilton steelworkers (overwhelmingly male) reduced or in jeopardy, a rising proportion of their partners sought employment or tried to increase their hours of paid work. While for most strata of the Hamilton population, the shift from a single-wage to a dual-earner family norm occurred fairly gradually over several decades, among the households of steelworkers the change-over was more abrupt. Based on labour force surveys, we estimate that in the mid 1970's roughly 70% of the co-resident wives of employed steelworkers in Hamilton were full-time homemakers. At the time of our interviews in 1984, that portion had declined to 42%. Our most recent estimate is that 80% are now employed.[9]

The decline of the male breadwinner norm unsettled conjugal relations, reduced women's economic dependence upon their husbands, dissolved an entrenched sense of the natural division of labour between spouses, and undercut men's customary prerogatives as breadwinners - above all, the right to treat the home as a leisure-centre, abstaining from housework and child-care. The mass influx of married women into paid work certainly eased the financial pressure on households. But it did so by adding very considerably to women's overall workload. This was a burden that they were very keen to get their husbands to share with them more equitably by substantially increasing the men's domestic contribution.

As mentioned, drastic downsizing has also disrupted the life-course and continuity between the generations. From the 1940's to the mid 1970's, thousands of young men entered Hilton Works in their teens, fresh out of high school; for many it was their first full-time job. Throughout this period, the labour force expanded in most years and hiring was more or less continuous in the coke-ovens and the blast furnace, the plant's "dirty-work" departments. Most recruits would make good money, save some and then quit within a year or two. But a significant minority of young workers hung on and ended up in the population from which our sample was drawn, eventually being promoted out of the worst (hottest, most hazardous and unskilled) jobs. With the protection of a strong union, job security and decent pay, they were able to get married, have kids and buy a house in their early to mid twenties.

As they contemplate the future today, many middle-aged respondents worry more about their children than their own fortunes in old age. They contrast their life-course with the prospects before youth now.

> When I started at Stelco in the late 1970's, I had worked at several manufacturing jobs and it was not a problem. It was apply for a job and you were hired. Kids can't do that now, not even coming out of university. Where are they getting their summer jobs? It's pumping gas someplace, or working at McDonald's? [1994, Male, ID# 78]

Within the core of the Canadian working-class, a sharp increase in economic insecurity has provoked serious questioning about people's established assumptions of class, gender, race and inter-generational relations. Before introducing our two couples and examining their views in depth, we need to explain the study's conceptual foundations.

Social Position and Group Awareness

The collective identities widely embraced in the late twentieth century - of class, nation, race, ethnicity and gender - have their distinct histories. Each has its own modes of assertion, mobilization and renewal; each must be studied in its particularity. While recognizing this imperative, what can be said *in general* concerning the foundations adequate to the study of different sorts of group identity-formation?

Group identities take shape around difference; we define ourselves in relation to the other. Gross disparities in power and wealth generate differences that almost invariably become antagonized and boundaried - us against them. In relations of conflict, collective identity-formation typically involves binary thinking, where the negative qualities stereotypically imputed to the other are an essential ground for casting ourselves in a positive light.[10] These bipolar contrasts, which serve to suppress awareness of diversity within groups and similarities between them, can not be explained simply in terms of discursive distortion and ideological hostility. They are generated through deep and long-standing conflicts of material interest between collectivities, based upon entrenched disparities of power and wealth between nations, classes, racial and ethnic groups, women and men. Such struggles provide a fruitful ground for discourses of exclusion, essentialism, blaming and victimization.

The social distinctions and hierarchies of class, gender, ethnicity and race cut across one another, placing us in society, and separating us from one another, in various ways. In jettisoning a class-reductive framework in favour of a more fluid, multidimensional perspective, we are not required to relinquish a materialist explanation of the main forms of group consciousness in evidence today. People are socially grouped, in the first place, by how they are placed in society and treated by others. The ways in which their subjectivity is discursively constituted is an important dimension of this process, but the *entire* process cannot be clearly apprehended in these terms. People are the social bearers of their basic identities; they are unable to shed them like so many costumes to pass for someone else. This intractability is especially binding for physically embodied and visible differences, such as race and gender.

The members of a nation, class, race or gender do not need to be friends, have similar backgrounds or daily lives, to make common cause with one another. In a world where people are often subject to similar treatment, hardship or risk, improvements are frequently best obtained by working together, and can often *only* be secured through joint action. Many people who do not otherwise have much in common may recognize an opportunity for collective benefit or common defence when they find their interests threatened by the same enemy, or many antagonists arrayed in parallel positions endeavouring to impose similar conditions upon them. Communication is indispensable. People become conscious of a shared interest through an exchange of information and views. As distinct interpretations are pooled, an overall assessment emerges and various responses to the situation are considered. We shall explore more fully below the role of communication in the formation and development of collective consciousness.

The multifaceted identities engendered by multidimensional structures of inequality are not fixed in a hierarchy of personal worth. Nor is there, in our view, any inexorable trend which will result in one of these identities strengthening and becoming an axis of decisive social struggle, while others are destined to decline and eventually disappear. No such predestined logic, or *telos,* may be imputed to the course of history.[11] Twenty years ago, most analysts figured that ethnic identity (with its pre-modern origins) was bound to recede in popular consciousness under the impact of globalizing trends such as the growth of television, rising international migration, and the domination lish as the language of world commerce. Instead, the opposite has occurred, largely as a reaction ***against*** these forces of cultural homogenization and ethnic intermixture. This unexpected result ought to provide a warning against extrapolating overarching logics into the future without regard to the complex interplay between global trends and local resistance to them. We shall examine below the error of classical marxism in predicting that class struggle would become the overriding axis of conflict in the Twentieth Century.

While people's identities are normally multifaceted, in situations of conflict, one identity can effectively submerge others. An intense strike may make union brothers and sisters of men and women from different racial backgrounds who formerly had very little to say to one another. Marxists were not wrong to recognize this potential. The mistake lay in underestimating the capacity of non-class cleavages to come to the fore - national divisions, for example. In Belgrade during the recent NATO bombing campaign, a professional woman who had long opposed the Milosevic government's policies told a Western reporter, "Before this war, I was a woman, a psychologist, a wife, a mother. Now I am primarily a Serb. I have been reduced to that." [12] In *The Warrior's Honour*, Michael Ignatieff asks,

> how identities that were once permeable begin to be sealed off. How did people begin to think of themselves as Serbs and Croats to the exclusion of all else? For nearly fifty years, being a Serb or a Croat took second place to being Yugoslav; sometimes it took third or fourth place to being a worker or a mother, or any of the other identities that constitute the range of our belonging...(p. 45). Now as he sits in his farmhouse bunker, there are men two hundred and fifty yards away who would kill him. For them, he is only a Serb, not a neighbour, not a friend, not a Yugoslav, not a former teammate at the football club. And because he is only a Serb for his enemies, he is only a Serb to himself. (p. 38).

These other identities will not remain sealed off forever; as the conflict abates and life returns to normal, they reemerge. It remains an open question, however, whether inter-ethnic bonds of association at the local level (as good neighbours, teammates, in-laws and so on) will ever be restored to their former levels of trust. It seems more likely that these other identities, and the social relations that foster them, will be confined for decades within ethnic bounds, especially for those who were combatants or victims in the conflict. In this way, one axis of group affiliation and identity comes to limit others without however suppressing them for long.

Elaborating the Classical Materialist Thesis

Within this framework, informed by cultural theory, what sense do we make of the classical materialist assertion that social being determines consciousness?[13] Consider three aspects:

1. Just as people observing a physical object from divergent vantage points will see it differently, so too will the participant-observers of a social process. People's locations in a communication field determine the information they routinely receive.

2. People who occupy a given position within a company, family or community are constrained to conduct themselves in certain ways. Their options are limited by the situation they find themselves in and by the routine responsibilities imposed upon them. In striving to become competent in the performance of their duties, they develop specific forms of utilitarian knowledge. Pragmatic knowledge of this sort is intimately related to viewpoint: managers, for example, value technocratic knowledge, conducting top-down surveys of their departments' operations, assessing various performance measures. They think about the organization, and direct its staff, in light of this knowledge.

3. People typically seek to justify their actions, to themselves and to others, by reference to the responsibilities of their position. If criticized, they are inclined to defend their actions by claiming that they had no real alternative but to do what

they did. In the process, they fuse, and confuse, their identity with their station. The powerful will typically motivate harsh measures for subordinates as "necessary medicine" for their own good, while the relatively powerless will often argue that they had to comply, given the consequences of defiance. In societies where there are huge disparities of wealth and power which cannot be legitimized by reference to birth and breeding, this self-justification will tend to generate a meritocratic explanation for the reproduction of inequality.

In these ways - through observation, pressures to conform, and self-justifying rationales for action, - people come to see the world from the vantage point of their position and to act accordingly. This hypothesis does not require a cynical or Machiavellian view of human nature. It assumes the normal operation of self-interest and the propensity to project one's own interests onto the community-at-large. Most of the time, people sincerely believe that whatever benefits them is consistent with the general welfare of the whole organization or society in the long run.

The "being-determines-consciousness" postulate offers a compelling account of many persistent aspects of consciousness. Consider, for example, the well-known phenomenon of people changing their tune as they rise through the ranks of an organization or take on a very different assignment. We are familiar with the vitriolic speeches of opposition Members of Parliament who are quick to find fault with everything the government does. Then, after an election, when these same people take up residence on the government side of the House, they end up justifying policies and actions they had previously denounced. These predictable turnabouts smack of rank hypocrisy and opportunism; they account, in part, for a widespread public perception that politicians are liars and deceivers. But *are* politicians, by nature, more hypocritical than the rest of us? Would it not be more insightful to offer a materialist account of their evolving consciousness as their objective position changes? In the first place, what do politicians find it ***necessary to say*** in order to get elected; secondly, what are they ***required to do*** to govern; and finally, what do they ***need to say to account for what they have done*** to remain in office? These are much tougher questions, directing attention to the weak accountability in our electoral form of government and the image-driven nature of contemporary politics. It is easier, and more superficial, to blame politicians for breaking their promises and betraying the people who elected them. In less dramatic terms, as we shall see below, our working-class respondents also "change their tune" as their circumstances change.

A defensible version of the being-determines-consciousness hypothesis would hold that ***the context-specific views of most people who come to occupy similar positions in an organization will tend to converge over time***. Note five ways in which this claim is qualified.

1. We do not say all views, but simply those ***directly related to the institutional context*** in which people find themselves. The effect of their association on other matters will be more diffuse, their views more likely to remain divergent.

2. We refer to ***most*** people, not all, because there are typically some people who are isolates or who hold an unyielding set of beliefs not amenable to change through the influence of new environments and the persuasion of associates.

3. We say people are placed in ***similar***, not identical, positions in a social field, sharing many features, risks and opportunities, resources and prerogatives around which a collective sense of being "in the same boat" can be built.

4. We do not claim that most people will come to hold identical views, but simply that their context-related views will ***tend to converge*** over time. This does not ensure a uniform outcome. There may be contrary forces at work that are sufficiently powerful to prevent confluence. Within a multicultural work force experiencing rapid labour turnover, for example, racial hostility or cultural incomprehension may keep various groups of employees from discussing their working conditions with one another and acting in concert to confront their employer. In this context, gradual convergence may never result in the majority seeing eye to eye on what constitutes decent working conditions and fair employment practices.

5. While divisive forces may overwhelm the tendency to convergence for a time, they will not eradicate it. When counteracting pressures abate (when, in the case described above, labour turnover slows, racial tensions ease, and friendships form between people in various groups) those in similar positions will begin to (re)discover common interests and shared perceptions. We therefore postulate the convergent tendency as a *persistent and general* phenomenon.

The development of like-mindedness is thus understood as a complex and mediated process. Whether people who come to see themselves as being aligned are able to take effective action to assert their interests is a distinct, though closely related, question; we shall address it below.

Amending the Classical Materialist Thesis

Let us now offer six friendly amendments to the being-determines-consciousness thesis to extend its application. Then we will proceed to register some more serious objections that require, in our view, thorough-going revisions.

1. The thesis argues *from* a similarity of objective condition *to* the formation of collective consciousness. Without abandoning this premise, we can propose that *cause and effect operate in a reciprocal fashion* via the activity of those involved. In many cases, people who become aware of a shared risk or opportunity decide to pool their resources and bind their individual fortunes together by forming an association dedicated to the furtherance of their joint interests. In the case of trade unions, for example, collective bargaining fortifies the underlying commonality of the workers condition by imposing a unitary contract upon an entire work force. In this way, the workers' solidarity and struggle modifies their material conditions, strengthening common aspects of their situation.

2. While marxists have emphasized the exterior moment in the formation of collective consciousness (conflict with an op-

posing group or class) we should also note the importance of *friendship, sharing, support and solidarity* among kin, neighbours and work-mates in promoting a sense of cultural affinity and shared values among a community. While the collective's identity may be extra-local, the interior bonds of group adhesion are maintained, for the most part, in face-to-face relations of caring and consideration. These forms of support are crucial antidotes to feelings of insecurity and isolation engendered by economic dislocation and market atomism.

3. In shifting our attention from local association to spatially extended affiliation on a regional, national or international basis, we need to appreciate the decisive importance of accessible *vehicles of group assertion*, so that people can envision ways of working together with others they have never met, and probably never will meet, to improve their situation. Again, trade unions have been the most evident examples among working-class people. Particularly in the past decade, the feminist movement has become more fully international, with multilateral links established around the world at conferences such as the U.N. Women's Conference in Beijing.

4.Working-class people are renowned as pragmatists. But this does not imply the existence of some sort of universal common-sense which is manifest everywhere by down-to-earth working folk. We reject the assumption that material circumstances dictate specific courses of action, furnishing the basis for a practical rationality that operates beneath the higher realms of culture and subjectivity. Since people are immersed in the culture in which they make decisions, *all forms of calculative rationality are culture-specific*. Cultural norms are particularly important in standardizing responses while making alternative actions seem inconceivable, ridiculous or deeply shameful. The availability of an option is thus both a matter of practical access to it and its recognition as a possible course of action. It is often illuminating *to distinguish* objective constraints which are beyond a person (or group's) immediate control from subjective obstacles which prevent someone from considering all the possible alternatives; but it is a mistake to *separate out* the material and ideological dimensions of social structure.

5. The assumption that individuals ally with others and act collectively in order to advance their interests is a valid generalization, but it should not be construed in a narrowly individualist and hyper-rationalist way. When we do this, we are left with *homo economicus,* the economists favourite abstraction, maximizing his or her utility in a competitive market context. As well as needing to "put food on the table," people in all societies, even thoroughly capitalist ones, *strive to be recognized and respected by others.*[14] This point should not be too difficult for English-speaking Canadians to grasp confronted with the state-breaking potential of the Quebec people's struggle for recognition as a nation. Even in industrial strikes where economic objectives are paramount, the conflict will intensify when workers' sense of fairness is violated, when they feel that management takes them for granted or pays them no respect. Such intangibles are normally blended with considerations of material well-being when people assert their interests and assess their options. Among those who devote themselves unstintingly to a cause, take risks and make sacrifices, firm bonds of loyalty tend to develop very rapidly. No realistic model of group belonging and collective action can afford to ignore the human need for recognition and the emotional foundations of affiliation.

6. Group adhesion is too often conceived as something occurring over a relatively short period of time. Enduring forms of group membership and solidarity are often sustained *for decades and centuries* by feelings of kinship, an awareness of common heritage and shared history passed down from generation to generation. Collective memory is constantly being refreshed by story-telling, flag-waving, songs, anniversary remembrances, and the display of badges of group identity. Climactic struggles and historic turning points, long ago, become the reference points of heroic myth. Even when they have long been in recession and seem to be forgotten, collective memories will be suddenly rediscovered with the revival of an impulse to group action.

Towards a Multifaceted Version of Group Consciousness

We turn now to more fundamental problems. Marxists have traditionally advanced a unilateral conception of self-interest, positing a true interest shared by people in a common condition. Members of the group in question who were not inclined to see it the same way were held to be the victims of false consciousness. Workers who collaborated with their bosses were routinely derided as dupes of bourgeois propaganda, having fallen under the sway of alien class influences. This diagnosis has not been unique to marxists; feminists have often made similar characterizations of backward,"male-identified" women.

People may, of course, have false ideas about their situation, especially about the position and intent of others. But far from *preventing* them from recognizing and acting upon their true interests (as the standard notion of false consciousness implies), these errors often make it *easier* for people to act in self-serving ways in so far as they permit them to believe that their actions are based upon higher, more honourable, motives. Consider racist reasoning, for example. It is false to mentally divide the world's people into different races and attribute widely different innate dispositions and abilities to them. But in accounting for the actual distribution of life's rewards and opportunities, it may be in our interest to believe that. If, as white men, the authors were to find ourselves in a job competition with black applicants (or women) and end up getting the job, we would like to believe that we won on our merits and not because the employer discriminated against black candidates. If, on the other hand, we lost to a black (or woman), it may be convenient to believe that the competition was biased, that affirmative action policies determined the result. In either case, it is easiest to think about the situation in a self-serving way. People with high social status would like to believe that their relative success in the world is due to their own efforts, honesty, diligence, or whatever. That's perfectly understandable, and by no means unique to affluent white men! But it does mean that more inclusive reasoning (anti-racist, anti-sexist) is often difficult to sustain because it rubs against the grain of our own narrow and immediate interests in looking out for Number One.

Classical marxism did offer other, more insightful, explanations for the failure of workers to develop class consciousness. Wilhelm Reich (1946) placed the emphasis on childhood upbringing in patriarchal families. He postulated that repressive and puritanical fathers would tend to produce children who were passive-aggressive towards authority. This could lead people, later in life, to project their aggression downward onto the most vulnerable members of society in the absence of opportunities to channel their anger upward against the ruling class. Lenin furnished another type of explanation entirely when he argued that the enormous superprofits of imperialism, based upon the superexploitation of the labourers of poor countries, enabled capitalists in rich countries,

> to bribe the labour leaders and the upper layers of the labour aristocracy... This stratum of workers-turned-bourgeois ... who are quite Philistine in their mode of life, in the size of their earnings and in their entire outlook ... are the real agents of the bourgeoisie in the workers movement. (Lenin, 1970, p. 677).[15]

If taken seriously, this boldly materialist thesis would have thrown into doubt the core premise of marxist orthodoxy - that the proletarians of *all* countries had a compelling interest in uniting to overthrow capitalism. It was a particularly devastating hypothesis in so far as the major trade unions were largely based in the upper layers of the working-class.

In our view, the big problem with the orthodox marxist conception of class consciousness is that people's material interests are typically conflicted in *all* class, race and gender positions. Workers have an interest in fighting capital to improve their wages and working conditions; they also have an interest in co-operating with their employers in order to protect their jobs. Women have an interest in fighting for equal pay; but, as cohabiting partners, they also have a stake in their husbands' paycheck which may serve to reinforce their own economic dependence. And so on. Reasonable people, acting rationally, normally have several possible ways to interpret their situation and to advance their interests.

1. They may decide to act individually or collectively.

2. They may wish to act collectively, but be unable to agree on the objectives of joint action. Some people will have a short-term orientation; others will set their sights on far-reaching goals.

3. Even when they agree on basic goals, the members of a group may differ over strategy and tactics. Whenever the outcome of a conflict is difficult to foresee, reasonable people will differ in their estimate of the chances of various courses of action succeeding.

4. People may possess different information about their joint situation due to different vantage points, information sources and social networks.

5. "Facing reality" undoubtedly limits the alternatives; rarely does it rule out all but one. If several courses of action may be rationally pursued, then there is no *a priori* reason why the calculation of advantage will consistently favour one over others. Everything depends on how people construe their self-interest within the limits set by forces and circumstances beyond their control.

6. Approaching a situation with varied life-experiences, people have different risk-reward temperaments. Some may be inclined to act defensively to maintain their prerogatives under the present regime, while others are willing to take greater risks in an attempt to change the system.

7. People may employ different comparative standards in assessing their fortunes. Some steelworkers we interviewed felt fortunate to be employed by Stelco because they were paid better than most workers in the city; others were outraged that Stelco managers received huge performance bonuses while claiming that the company could not afford to meet their own relatively modest pay demands. The first comparison fosters contentment; the second labour militancy. Often both views were held by the same individual. In this case, the person's disposition will depend upon which measuring stick predominates when group action is being contemplated.

In view of this diversity, how is collective action possible?

There will often be compelling circumstances (such as a brutal attack by a clearly identifiable opponent) that induce large numbers to conclude that collective action is urgently required to defend their vital interests. A shared sense of fear and anger may be felt by many observers, virtually simultaneously. But rarely do they then proceed, like a school of fish, to move *en masse* in the same direction. Mass movements are not inchoate mobs. Often, they congeal very quickly and their sudden appearance takes everyone by surprise, including their own members; but they never arise spontaneously. As Charles Tilly and others have shown, they come together on the basis of preexisting social networks of trust and solidarity; these are vital in stitching together a collectivity.[16] Then they must discuss their options. Large numbers of potential participants must feel that the group is capable of effective mobilization; a persuasive case must be made for a course of action that most find acceptable. Finally, people must be sufficiently convinced of the dangers of *failing* to act collectively that most are prepared to set aside their differences, subordinate their individual priorities and act in concert, if only for a limited time.

When people are ambivalent - torn between a conservative risk-averse response and a grievance-identified combative course of action - the decisive variable is often how they see the future unfolding. If they believe that the insurgent force is destined to win, they have a strong reason to throw in their lot with an opposition whose grievances and basic goals they share. The rapid swelling of a mass movement is generally based upon an increasing confidence in its ability to win. If, on the other hand, the fight seems an exercise in futility, and especially if reprisals are feared, then the prudent course of action is to keep your head down or to ally with the authorities. As soon as a pessimistic appraisal becomes commonplace, support will drain away just as rapidly as it arose in the first place. Since perceptions of the likelihood of victory or defeat change over time, it may be rational for most workers to support a strike while it is strong, but admit defeat and return to work when it appears that nothing more can be gained by continued defiance. There will typically be some who will oppose collective action from

main adamant that the struggle should be continued as a matter of principle even though it appears to be going down to defeat. But the majority in the middle are likely to be situationally sensitive to the prospects for success or failure and respond accordingly.[17]

Objective Interest and Subjective Identity

As many left-wing intellectuals abandoned marxism for postmodernist discourse theories, personal identity displaced material interest as the imputed foundation of social awareness and group belonging. While the cultural articulation of gender, sexual orientation, nationality and race were extensively analyzed, social class came to be treated as if it were *passé*. In part, this was due to a conjunctural decline in strikes and unionization, but it was also because social class is less embodied than race or gender. In a style of analysis preoccupied with the "inscription of discourses upon the body," the calculation of material interests was radically downplayed (see Butler, 1993).

While we are skeptical about the linguistic turn, we refuse to accept an either/or contrast between material interest and cultural identity. The objective must be synthesis. We may dislike the ways in which most postmodernists approach identity-formation, but it was valid for them to insist upon the importance of doing so and quite correct to criticize orthodox marxists for largely failing to do so, simply deriving true group-consciousness from unitary interests.

In so far as people's social location and their inner sense of self both impinge upon consciousness and co-determine behaviour, the imprint of neither can be well understood without taking serious account of the other. All reality-based assessments of social context are read through personal identity and alternatives for action are weighed accordingly. Conversely, personal identity is grounded in one's objective location and is constantly being reformed by realistic adaptions to it.[18]

We need not discount the persistent influence of people's location and current circumstances upon their consciousness in order to take seriously the subjective conditions of group iden-

order to take seriously the subjective conditions of group identity-formation. This is just as true of gender and race as it is of class. All are objective social locations in the world, assigned at birth and normally conveyed by families in the process of growing up. In the case of race and gender, they are imputed to be genetically encoded group attributes which give rise to significant disparities in innate abilities and dispositions. This is profoundly deceptive. The measurable differences are actually slight and the biggest ones are skin-deep (visible on the body's surface); the rest cannot possibly account for the profound inequalities between these groups in modern societies. Sharp disparities in life-chances indicate that gender and race are, fundamentally, socially assigned birth-locations that appear to take the form of personal attributes. They are not unlike social class in this regard. But being personally embodied, they are more deeply naturalized and less alterable over the life-course by means of social mobility. A black woman (exceptionally) may rise from the shop floor to become a supervisor; in doing so, she hikes her income, enhances her corporate authority, and improves her class location; but she does not cease to be black and female. If she is tempted to forget these persistent facts of life, others will doubtless remind her.

As there is discretionary scope for the rational pursuit of self-interest and group-allegiance along several lines, people's motives for acting as they do will normally involve the affirmation of personal identity. Presented with several realistic options that appear to be equally attractive (or objectionable), one is inclined to choose the path of least *subjective* resistance, aligning one's prospects for situational advantage with what "feels right," or is "my obligation under the circumstances," (the latter often entailing group loyalty). If, on the other hand, the objective situation clearly favours one course over others, then contrary subjective dispositions will generally be subdued by a process of internal rationalization.

This perspective allows for identity-affirming motives to be consciously considered, becoming part of the deliberative process; they may also function as subconscious drives originating in childhood that predispose us, as adults, to repeat certain behaviour patterns. Cultural critics are often preoccupied with unconscious drives that induce us to act in irrational, self-destructive ways. But, under most circumstances, adults are able to reconcile impulse with the rational pursuit of self-interest. Freud conceived of this reality-based adaptive process through his famous tripartite conception of personality structure: in healthy adults, a strong and competent Ego effectively integrated the Id (primitive desires) with the Superego (moral conscience). Others, such as Piaget, have proposed alternative paradigms.[19] Regardless of how we conceive of character-formation, the socialization of children must achieve an integration in all societies so that people can develop a cumulative sense of identity prior to puberty and then consolidate it in the transition to adulthood. Without such an adaption to the reality-principle, (in Freud's words), the maintenance of social order would be impossible; even attempts at organized rebellion would dissolve in chaos.[20] While youth socialization is a universal requisite of inter-generational reproduction, the process has become increasingly difficult in recent decades. The rapid pace of technological and cultural change outmodes traditional experience and undermines the older generation's capacity to convey personally-based pragmatic knowledge that young people might find useful. This tends to erode the respect that adolescents evince for the wisdom of their elders.

Dimensions of Social Subordination and Inequality

Classical marxism was preoccupied with the formation of class consciousness in large work-places where workers were unionized. This focus was developed in the service of a strategic vision that was premised upon forging proletarian unity as the only way in which the power of capital could be effectively challenged and overthrown. The general strike, led by the "big battalions of labour," was the prototypical form of this revolutionary response from below. Other fundamental social divisions and inequalities were taken up as questions (the national question, the woman question, the black question, and so on), reflecting their vexed nature within the revolutionary project.

Socialists recognized that the fight for the democratic demands of these groups could jeopardize working-class unity if they were not effectively embraced by the labour movement and incorporated in the political programs of its leading parties. To their credit, many devoted great effort to securing this support, although they underestimated how difficult it would be, given the competitive divisiveness fostered by capitalism.

Optimistically, Marx had anticipated that the main non-class divisions would become less salient as the ranks of the proletariat swelled and international capitalism eroded the traditional occupational segregation of craft, trade and skill which had hampered the formation of an inclusive class consciousness.

> With the development of industry, the proletariat not only increases in number; it becomes concentrated in greater masses, its strength grows, and it feels that strength more. The various interests and conditions of life within the ranks of the proletariat are more equalized, in proportion as machinery obliterates all distinctions of labour and nearly everywhere reduces wages to the same low level... Modern subjection to capital, the same in England as in France, in America as in Germany, has stripped [the worker] of every trace of national character. Law, morality, religion are to him so many bourgeois prejudices, behind which lurk in ambush just as many bourgeois interests.(1974a, pp. 75, 79)

As it turned out, Marx's prediction of proletarian homogenization and increasing internationalism was wishful thinking. Capital's perpetual motion, and labour's flexibility in response, *did* strip away occupational and trade barriers to work-place integration. The decline of the protectionist craft unions and the rise of more inclusive industrial unions, organized nationwide, was facilitated by these processes. Furthermore, great advances in travel, communication, and mass literacy enabled working people, for the first time in history, to overcome the parochialism endemic in their situation and to create national and international associations through which they could learn from one another, co-ordinate their struggles, and develop a global perspective on how best to advance their collective interests. However, Marx's vision of horizontal co-operation from below was undermined, in the final analysis, by deep and enduring divisions which congealed in the formation and growth of the proletariat.[21]

The global extension of capitalism did not make the nation-state less important for workers, as Marx had predicted. The advent of universal adult suffrage and the construction of the Welfare State in the Twentieth Century have heightened the national consciousness of proletarian citizens. Working people looked increasingly to their own state for protection from multinational corporations and foreign investors. Within states, the creation of a national labour market and the ascendant power of employers to hire individuals according to their own criteria broadened the field of competition among proletarians for the best available jobs, laying bare the inequities of race and gender discrimination in stratifying the working-class. Among the upper layers of the regularly employed labour force, overwhelmingly white men, breadwinner insecurity was exacerbated as their job niches eroded. Increasingly, they came to fear and resent the competition of women, immigrants and racial minorities whose poverty made them a ready source of cheap-labour replacement. Employers and established workers usually colluded in the re-segmentation of the labour force along race and gender lines. While constantly warning workers about the dangers of the bosses' divide-and-conquer tactics, marxists nonetheless clung to a bi-polar, "zero-sum" understanding of class conflict, seriously underestimating the leeway that employers had to offer their better paid and more technically skilled workers deals that would significantly alleviate their insecurities while simultaneously increasing inequalities across the labour force as a whole.

Unable to reconcile the reality of these intra-class divisions with their belief in the universal proletariat, marxists squared the circle with an idealist argument concerning false consciousness and bitter denunciations of labour leaders for betraying the workers true , revolutionary, interests. In the first place, they typically equated the trade union movement with the working-class. In most capitalist countries, unions organize only a minority of the wage-earning class, and the parties of the working-class do not regularly obtain a majority of the votes cast by the proletarian electorate. While steadfastly seeking to broaden the workers' movement and reach out to the oppressed, marxists none the less proceeded *as if* the good intentions of a minority of progressive workers who shared this inclusive vision would suffice to overcome the privileged position of the protectionist majority of the industrial core. In reality, the latter's interest in preventing the poor, minorities and women from gaining competitive access to their sectors was materially based and not simply a form of false consciousness.

There is a nest of closely related problems here. For the purposes of clarification, let us distinguish three strands.

1. The elevation of class and the correlated downgrading of other dimensions of social subordination and inequality.

2. The fixation on the point of production, while virtually ignoring the other spheres of daily life, especially households, but also shops, restaurants, pubs, streets, parks and community centres.

3. The narrow focus on the exploitation of the regularly employed labour force. The bottom layers of the proletariat - the wage-hungry job-seekers who are marginalized or shut out entirely - were peripheral to the orthodox field of vision.

As we have argued above, "being determines consciousness" is an adequate starting point *providing* we remain open to the reality that social being is multi-sited, people's interests are multilateral and often conflicted, their loyalties divided. As materialists, we insist that these conflicts are objectively given; they do not stem from confusion, misperception or ambivalence. Frequently, however, they give rise to such troubling states of mind, and precisely because they *are* psychologically uncomfortable, people will normally strive to reconcile contradictory inclinations and develop internal consistency so that they can make up their minds and justify their actions to themselves and to others. In the process of internal rationalization, they may simplify their position and distort the situation of others, rendering themselves susceptible to demagogic appeals and hostile projection upon vulnerable populations. In recognizing the impact of mass ideological persuasion, however, we should not imply that they have become incapable of recognizing and acting upon their own interests. The reality is that by articulating their interests narrowly along certain fault-lines while eschewing more inclusive up-from-under alternatives, they have followed the path of least resistance. This is why it is so difficult to move beyond a generally expressed sentiment of group-belonging to take sustained and effective action along any given axis of collective identity. To do so, "we the people" must set aside our very real differences and resist the temptation to try to improve our fortunes in the short term at the expense of others below us in the hierarchy.

Core-Periphery Dynamics of the Proletariat

As outlined above, marxism's traditional focus has been on the exploitation of subordinated producers toiling at the heart of a mode of production - of peasants toiling for landlords, slaves for their owners, and workers for capitalists. This framework was inhospitable to an analysis of marginalization which appeared to take place *outside* the mode of production in question.

Under capitalism, integrated subordination and economic marginalization are two sides of the proletarian condition. On the negative side, *all* proletarians lack income from capital or other means of livelihood, so they need to seek wage work in order to subsist. On the positive side, *most* manage to obtain employment and their households generate a sufficiently steady stream of wage income to be able to live "decently" (a cultural construct which the respectable members of a working-class community can reasonably expect to attain). What of the others, unable to secure regular employment?[22] Their marginality is not simply economic. Those who are culturally exterior to the nation's mainstream usually find it difficult to secure regular employment at decent pay-rates for reasons that have little to do with their job credentials or performance abilities.

While race relations vary from country to country, what is nonetheless striking is the *generality of the correlation between economic and cultural marginalization*: between poverty and residential ghettoisation, the colour of people's skin and the types of jobs they have a reasonable chance of obtaining.[23]

We can see this internationally in the North-South relationship between rich and poor countries, where the work of Immanuel Wallerstein (1979) and his associates has been instructive. But even within highly industrialized Western nations, core-periphery dynamics are evident, as economic and cultural forces reinforce one another. Typically, race relations become increasingly strained as unemployment mounts and the poor intensify their search for scarce jobs. For our (mostly white) respondents in the traditional core of the English-Canadian working-class, the economic danger is clear and terrifying as they watch former work-mates and in some cases their own children sinking into poverty, unable to find steady jobs. Even as they express strong support for trade unions and the rights of labour in collective bargaining, they think of themselves as middle-class because they can see that they are in the middle with a yawning gap between themselves, the rich above, and the poor below. As times get tougher and the fear of falling intensifies, they find themselves increasingly looking down, aware of the stark contrast between their own positions and those on the bottom of the heap, often from minority groups.

The proletarian dialectic between integration and marginalization is crucial in comprehending the foundation of racial and ethnic stratification in capitalist nation-states. Most modern nations have been built around a "vertical mosaic," where the core of the propertied and professional classes constitute an ethno-cultural mainstream to which certain members of the class of wage earners can assimilate, while others, more visibly different, are persistently marginalized. Even though Canada is now formally a multicultural country, it is still constituted around two founding cultures, English and French, who settled and grew by forcibly displacing the aboriginal peoples. In English Canada, the upper class of the nation's traditionally dominant group has been dubbed "the WASP establishment." Members of the middle-class and the upper layers of the working-class who are of Northwestern European descent have been assimilated into this ethno-cultural mainstream. Today, the vast majority think of themselves as "just Canadian." Southern and Eastern Europeans, arriving in Canada later, found the process of incorporation more difficult, and hence gradual; most were assimilated in a few generations, although a significant minority still think of themselves as ethnic (or "hyphenated") Canadians. The Chinese (recruited originally to work on the trans-Canada railway) and, more recently, immigrants from the Caribbean and South Asia were increasingly admitted as the supply of white immigrants dried up. Despite their desire to become Canadian, they often find it difficult to integrate. Both in English Canada and Quebec, they have remained on the margins of the national mainstream, frequently suffering racist rebuffs.

This racial and ethnic layering is interwoven with, and sustained by, economic inequalities from top to bottom, both between and within classes. By breaking with the traditional marxist viewpoint which focuses simply on the integrated core of the regularly employed proletariat, we can analyze a broader field of socio-economic *positions*. This lays the groundwork for integrating a cultural analysis of the movement of *living agents* who come to Canada and take their places on the periphery of the working-class.[24]

1. The classical marxist thesis concerning the reserve army of labour (RAL) is relevant here. In the history of capitalism, mass unemployment has been the norm; periods of full employment have been unusual. Marx argued that the key factor in explaining unemployment is not population growth or a government's immigration policy. The expulsion of labour from production is a normal by-product of technological innovation and capital accumulation; in the competitive drive to cut costs and shore up profits, firms raise productivity through labour-displacing technological change (Marx, 1967, pp. 589-606). The unemployed facilitate capital accumulation in three related ways:

1. Providing masses of people keen to work for wages, readily available to go to work at a day's notice, and willing to travel to places where companies are hiring. The responsiveness of this surplus population is especially important in periods of rapid expansion. In times of stagnation, they represent the "last hired, first fired," relatively easy for employers to dismiss.

2. The existence of a substantial body of unemployed workers tilts the balance of class forces in the employers' favour. By competing for jobs at every level of the labour force, the unemployed bid down the price of labour and act as an external prod to the employed, who are reminded that others are "out there," keen to replace them, willing to work for less pay, and prepared to put up with inferior working conditions. The unemployed enforce labour discipline, compelling the employed to prove their worth to their employers continually.

3. The expansion and contraction of the RAL is an important equilibrating factor in the business cycle. During boom periods (e.g., from 1940 to 1972 in Canada), job growth is strong, unemployment declines, labour's bargaining power is fortified, real wages rise, profits are eventually squeezed, the boom peters out, and a slowdown ensues. In subsequent phases of economic stagnation (e.g., from 1973 to 1991), relatively little job growth occurs, unemployment rises, labour s position is weakened and capital cuts costs more aggressively. As productivity rises, real wages stagnate or decline, profit rates recover, reinvestment surges, and economic growth quickens once again.[25]

In the protracted slowdown from the mid 1970's on, ruthless cost-cutting by firms striving to remain competitive led to massive layoffs and rising unemployment rates across the developed capitalist world. This was accompanied by the drive of governments to restrain the growth of state social expenditure by cutting transfers to the poor and unemployed. These measures made the latter increasingly desperate to find employment, intensifying the competition for scarce jobs. Rapid technological change, high unemployment and government cutbacks all served to make the employed more insecure. Averting layoffs became their primary consideration. In this context, they were more receptive to management appeals to work harder and accept wage cuts to keep the company in business, weakening their bargaining power in the process. The unemployed thus play an important role in the drive of metropolitan capital towards global competitiveness.

Women have served as a major labour reserve for employers. Except in periods of high demand, notably in wartime, most have been relegated to certain stereotypically "female" sectors. The consolidation of the male-breadwinner family wage norm in the latter decades of the Nineteenth Century entrenched a strong division of labour among respectable working-class couples, where men were regularly employed and women left their jobs when they married, or soon after, to become full-time homemakers.[26] Among the lower strata of the working-class, among recent immigrants and racial minorities, it was rarely possible to sustain a one-wage family economy. Men from these groups were largely unable to obtain sufficient income on a steady basis, so women and children did all manner of work to make up the difference. To the respectable working-class families of the white-European mainstream, they appeared "rough" or "backward," their familial customs alien, their morals dubious.

Since the 1960's, Canadian women have made impressive gains in paid employment, with more and more sustaining participation throughout their childbearing years. Nowadays, when one applies for a job or seeks promotion, it is not supposed to matter whether one is a man or a woman. As our steelworker respondents repeatedly insisted, the only real issue is the worker's competence to do the job at hand. But even if the formal norms of the work-place downplay the difference, systemic inequities persist; the worker's gender remains a potent consideration, not least upon their consciousness as workers. Whether women entering the previously male domain of a steel mill are welcomed, their skills recognized, and their contribution valued, will critically effect their capacity to identify with their fellow workers and develop an oppositional class consciousness which surmounts the gender divide.

Direct Experience, Life History and Present Views

Another materialist postulate we wish to retain is the primacy of first-hand experience in the formation of most people's world-views.[27] As David Lockwood states in his famous essay 'Sources of Variation in Working-Class Images of Society:'

> for the most part, men visualize the class structure of their society from the vantage points of their own particular milieu, and their perceptions of the larger society will vary according to their experiences of social inequality in the smaller societies in which they live out their lives. [28]

Our respondents align their general assessments of class, gender and race relations with their own first-hand experience, shaped by their personal relationships with family members, friends, work-mates and employers. News reports provide a sounding board for their views. They select, remember and recount facts and arguments from the range of news information and opinion on offer that reinforce their views and confirm their deepest feelings. Discordant facts and opinions tend to be discounted.

It will be useful here to distinguish between two adjacent realms of thought: a) practical consciousness arising from direct experience and the routine demands of everyday life, and b) considered reflection, distilled judgment, a philosophy of life, more likely to be articulated within broadly available public discourses and shaped by media presentation.[29] These mental registers utilize language and engage with the social world rather differently. While we have emphasized the role of direct experience in fostering group identification, the realm of reflective thought is perhaps where discourse analysis could be more usefully deployed.

There is, of course, nothing which keeps first-hand knowledge separate from remotely produced information. The raw input of sense-perception does not constitute a separate realm of personal knowledge apart from social context and the constant operation of language upon thought. They merge in the head. In this sense, we are always and inescapably immersed in the language and culture of a given community. In a text-dominated world, word-of-mouth is widely held to be inferior in the hierarchy of authorized knowledge. However, even in this multimedia Information Age, being a direct observer or an active participant in events, witnessing "with our own eyes" and hearing "with our own ears," makes such a deep impression upon emotion and memory that the sense we make of personal experience ought still to be accorded a general priority in the formation of social consciousness.

The visceral impact of television, however, blurs the distinction, since the presence of the camera makes the viewer a virtual eye-witness, and the sense of "being there" makes the voice-over narrative seem more like direct evidence than hear-say or interpretation. While through television we become aware of peoples in distant lands, (to be discussed further below), we are normally much more concerned with people in our immediate environment for the simple reason that their actions affect us directly in noticeable ways.

We take issue with postmodernist interpretations that discount life-experience as a category of naive naturalism and posit instead the primacy of text-mediated sources and authorized discourses in the formation of popular consciousness. Our disagreement is not simply what weight to accord personal experience and remotely mediated information in the formation of consciousness; obviously, they work in tandem. But in order to appreciate the ways they are combined, we need to deconstruct the notion of discourse itself, upholding basic distinctions between observation and conversation, direct experience and book-learning, personally conveyed information and news disseminated through the mass media. These distinctions are ignored in most versions of discourse analysis. Since all thought is rooted in and shaped by language, every facet of our consciousness is discursively constituted. From this undoubted truth, an implication is drawn that subordinated people are almost inevitably decentred by the hegemonic machinery of knowledge production, presumably incapable of developing a sustained critique of their society's dominant institutions.

The root of this conception, which separates language from the material world, is Saussure's insight that meaning is not produced in a one-to-one relationship between signifier and signified, between a word and its referent in the world beyond language, but is dependent upon the linguistic context. Meaning, in this view, is an effect of the movement from signifier to signifier, an operation entirely within the field of language.[30] This thesis was an over-reaction against an earlier naturalist view that considered language to be structured in transparent correspondence with the world beyond language, like a window pane transmitting images of what was going on outside.

Meaning is constituted in an ongoing dialectic between linguistic context and the impact of the world beyond language. Some forms of speech depend heavily on linguistic context; others are quite unambiguous as to their external referents. Not surprisingly, postmodernists have concentrated on the former. In literary fiction and film, for example, the narrative text creates a mental universe removed from reality; in these cases, the interior structure of language is clearly paramount in generating meaning. The problem is that theorists have applied the same principles of linguistic analysis to non-fictional forms of speech, including those that are pragmatically grounded in ongoing activities, such as conversation facilitating the routines of daily life.[31]

Just as thought is structured by language, speech is structured by the speaker's practical relation to the material world; most forms of human communication are "pinned down" by anchors to the world beyond language. Consistency of word selection in relating signifiers to the signified is essential to social intercourse. If we tell the immigration official that we intend to stay in the country two weeks and then return to depart after three, we may be asked to explain the discrepancy. In such a circumstance, we are not free to claim that "the seven-day week is an arbitrary construct and we have taken the liberty of redefining it." The meaning of week is discursively constituted, but it is simultaneously anchored in realities beyond language - in this case, in the diurnal rhythms of the natural world.

In studying extensive public discourses such as a nation's politics as covered by the media, careful attention must be paid to the ways in which they are taken up and reworked by people located in specific positions. They already have substantial commitments, interests and beliefs which have been formed over time; their thoughts on a given issue are not discursively constructed at a single point in time. People's views are a product of their history, the cumulative experience of a life-in-progress. Cultural heritage, family background, early life, primary schooling and religious training, (if any), the long process of gaining independence from one's parents are all crucial in the formation of an adult's character and temperament, his or her abiding beliefs and values. This seems so obvious, yet most sociological theories of public-opinion formation are notoriously ahistorical. Longitudinal surveys, following a specific population through time, are an antidote to this problem, but the method is costly, painstaking and underutilised. Even in one-time surveys of people's attitudes, relevant information can be obtained on past history.[32]

The personal biographies of a collection of people who find themselves "in the same boat" are bound to be far more varied than their shared circumstances. In a world of extensive mobility, of immigration and urbanization, the family backgrounds and personal biographies of people who eventually come to reside in the same neighbourhood or work together for the same employer are enormously diverse. These disparities often foster cultural incomprehension and indifference, making it difficult to develop a sense of shared history and group togetherness.

As adults, our past is a product of both choice and constraint. The choices we have made inevitably shape our present circumstances. Everyone has choices to make, but the poor and oppressed have fewer options available to them than the affluent and privileged, and their alternatives are worse, the trade-offs harsher. As parents, we are vitally concerned about the likely course of the future for our children. Our hopes and fears are fixed upon them. In tough times, inter-generational commitments can generate deep feelings of fear and anger especially for working-class parents who are unable to take care of their children by means of substantial inheritance, as the wealthy can. These generational issues will be discussed below.

The more sacrifices we make in pursuing one path while forgoing the opportunities of another, the more inclined we are to invest our chosen course with deep emotional meaning, turning our backs on the road-not-taken. We may agonize, for example, over the fateful decision to have a child, but as soon as the baby is born we strive to banish all doubts. It is little consolation, when changing diapers, to daydream of the holiday we would have taken if the baby had not arrived. Likewise, a mother who relinquishes her job to stay home and care for her young child may be particularly adamant that this was the right thing to do, disapproving of women who continue to work outside the home, placing their children in day-care. In this way, choice conditions material circumstances, which in turn shapes consciousness. The resulting correspondence between social position and consciousness is thus dialectically achieved.

The Core of the Working-Class: Steeltown Profiles

We have seen that the relationship between people's social position and their outlook is a complex and mediated one. Rarely will any large number of people in a similar position completely agree with one another, even on those issues that location most severely constrains. One might argue that this diversity proves that people s consciousness is simply too varied to have any persistent connection with the common conditions of their lives. Yet in a probabilistic estimate, the positioning of class, gender and family circumstances ***can*** account for a significant part of the variance in people s outlooks. Those who share a similar social location will be ***significantly more likely*** to hold certain views than those in different, and especially opposed, positions. The evidence from our empirical studies, cited below, confirms this.

In statistical analysis, researchers seek to increase the percentage of variance explained by introducing a number of mediating variables. For workers, the relationship between class position and labour consciousness is mediated by the presence or absence of a union, for example, and then (where unions are present) by the relative effectiveness of the union in defending its members' rights. By taking such factors into account, we increase our capacity to predict and explain the class-related views of a given population.[33]

Consider, for example, the estimates of oppositional class consciousness summarized in Table 2.

Table 2: Oppositional Class Consciousness in Hamilton, 1984

(Row Percentages)

Class Position	Oppositional Capitalist Consciousness %	Mixed-Class Consciousness %	Oppositional Working-Class Consciousness %	N
Ontario corporate executives	68	32	0	127
Small employers	40	56	4	44
Managers	41	44	15	48
Professionals	31	52	17	65
Supervisors	28	49	23	78
Self-employed	35	45	20	29
Working class	10	55	35	230
Unionized	9	53	38	113
Stelco workers	5	44	51	183
Stelco workers' spouses	10	45	45	183
Hamilton men	24	50	26	324
Hamilton women	23	59	20	170
Ontario population	23	67	9	1046

Sources
Ontario – Livingstone 1985: 54-57; Hamilton – Steelworker Families Survey 1984; Stelco workers and spouses – Hilton Works USWA 1005 Survey 1984. The class-specific results are aggregated here for both men and women in employment.

Oppositional class consciousness is measured here in terms of the rights of corporate owners to maximize their profits by investing wherever they choose, and the rights of employers to hire workers to take the place of striking employees.[34] The main finding from these 1984 surveys, confirmed by a continuing series of Ontario surveys, is that most people in most class positions express a mixed class consciousness (that is, they support profit maximization but oppose hiring scab workers, or they oppose profit maximization but support hiring scab workers, or they have uncertain views on one or both issues, (see Livingstone, 1987, pp. 194-212).

But the differences in these expressions of oppositional class consciousness according to class position are equally important. Corporate executives, who form the core of the capitalist class, are distinctive in their strong majority support for both profit maximization and the hiring of scab workers. While those in most class positions in Hamilton express either a mixed or divided class consciousness, the working-class is significantly less likely (only 10 per cent) to support both profit maximization and hiring scabs than those in any capitalist or intermediate class location. Hamilton's reputation as a working-class town is supported by the finding that its population is generally as likely to express a solid working-class consciousness (over 20 per cent) as a solid capitalist consciousness, whereas in Ontario overall capitalist consciousness is twice as likely as working-class consciousness. But even among Hamilton's unionized working-class, mixed class consciousness is at least as likely as a solid working-class consciousness. Only within the old core of the unionized working-class in large industrial work places such as Stelco's Hilton Works do we find a majority expressing a solid working-class consciousness in these terms. As Table 2 confirms, Stelco workers and their partners were among the most likely members of the Hamilton working-class to express a solid working-class consciousness in 1984.

We present profiles of two couples here, one young in 1984, the other middle-aged. All four individuals, with working-class backgrounds, have lived their entire lives in Hamilton. All are of British heritage and had limited formal schooling. All expressed a strong oppositional working-class consciousness in 1984 in terms of the above issues. Both couples remained together, and were interviewed together, ten years later.[35]

Dave and Donna

In 1984, Dave was a self-described "union radical" who had been very active in the Stelco local. As a middle-aged machine operator with over twenty years seniority, he was among the highest paid workers in the plant. On an alternating shift schedule, he had difficulty getting more than four or five hours of sleep a night or participating in any regular community activities. Dave did more household chores than most male steelworkers and also found time for some individual hobbies. He watched only a few hours of television per week. He had no religion. By 1994, Dave had retired from Stelco. In addition to his pension, he managed to pick up some consulting work in his area of specialization in the steel industry.

Donna was a homemaker working for pay part-time. She had been employed occasionally since her early marriage to Dave and had devoted herself primarily to caring for their children. She went back to paid work on a sustained, but still part-time basis during the 1981 Stelco strike, as a manual labourer in a communications company. She enjoyed her job, but expressed concern about the sexual harassment of younger women there. There was no union. She estimated doing about twice as much domestic labour as Dave, plus a lot of time in children s community activities and visiting relatives. She also slept a few more hours than Dave and watched a bit more television. She was an inactive mainstream Protestant. By 1994, Donna had taken upgrading training and was working regularly in a non-union semi-professional job. Their children had both graduated from college and left home.

Greg and Gilda

In 1984, Greg was one of the younger workers who remained at Stelco, in his mid-twenties but with over five years seniority. He had a basic labourer's job in the front-end of the plant (the blast furnace and coke ovens), with no skill qualifications and relatively low pay. He was particularly concerned about health hazards in his job but expressed no interest in the union. Working on alternating shifts, he could manage only about four hours of sleep per day. He spent quite a bit of time drinking after work with his buddies and was moderately active in a few community organizations. Greg helped out at home a fair bit, especially with his young children. He also watched a lot of television, at least a couple of hours a day. He attended a Protestant church but only rarely. By 1994, Greg had taken upgrading training and become a machine operator in the steel plant with a fairly secure job. His health and safety concerns had also led to his becoming a union activist. He was still working alternating shifts, but getting a few more hours of sleep and taking it in stride as something I got to do. He was also spending more time at home doing renovations and even more in local community organizations, and a lot less time with his drinking buddies.

Gilda was a young homemaker with small children. She had a full-time semi-skilled service job after high school and several similar part-time, non-union jobs since marriage, but in 1984 she was caring for a baby full-time. She was sleeping eight hours a night but rarely getting out of the house, except to attend regular services at a mainstream Protestant church. Her main recreations were having relatives visit or call on the phone, and watching television at least four hours a day. By 1994, Gilda had been employed again for several years in a regular four-days-a-week, non-union, service job, and had also become active as a church volunteer. She would still prefer to stay home with the kids, who are now teenagers.

Class Conflict and Class Consciousness

Marxists have typically coupled an emphasis on the importance of social location with an action premise. *Class consciousness is forged in the crucible of class struggles.*

In order to separate the valid kernel of this thesis from its more dubious extrapolations, let us begin by strictly distinguishing *structural contradictions* which generate a conflict of interest between groups from the struggles they engage in with one another.[36] Structural contradiction is an objective condition, roughly a zero-sum conflict, where the attempt of a group to advance its interests threatens to harm the interests of others. It is not a matter of consciousness; co-operative intent will not suffice to eliminate an endemic conflict of interest. Struggle, by contrast, is a deliberate act. We may say that a given group is forced to struggle because they are under attack, but the fact is that they do not begin to fight without being willing to do so; to move into overt action they must achieve a sense of antagonism towards an identifiable opponent.

In the traditional marxist argument, the generative structure of class conflict is not the prior consciousness of the combatants but the antagonisms built into the core structure of capitalist economies. In an intensely competitive environment (the normal condition of capitalism), profit-seeking firms are impelled to maximize labour's output while minimizing the payment necessary to sustain workers' productivity. The wage-earners interests are opposed. They toil for wages in order to live independently to secure, and wherever possible to enhance, their own living standards and the domestic comfort of their families, while limiting their own exertions on the employer's behalf. Whatever the conscious motivations of managers and workers, sooner or later this conflict takes on a zero-sum character: management's drive to cut costs and increase the value of labour's output threatens to worsen the working conditions and/or living standards of their employees.

In our view, the endemic labour-capital conflict thesis ought to be retained, not as a cherished article of faith, but because the evolution of capitalism in the late twentieth century amply confirms its reality. The prevalence of intense global competition between firms has induced corporate executives the world over to undertake severe cost-cutting measures which necessarily involve attempts to reduce real wages and roll back workers' established contractual rights and informal prerogatives. The objective contradictions in the process of capital accumulation which give rise to the collision of class interests between capital and labour is alive and well, especially in an era of "global restructuring."

If this relationship is bound to be conflicted, it is also, of necessity, co-operative. In order to preserve their jobs, workers depend on the private firms they work for to remain profitable and the public sector organizations who employ them to remain legitimate. The size of their future pay-cheques is circumscribed by the firm's future profitability, or in the case of public institutions, by maintaining government support for the institution's program. Most workers under capitalism are alienated from the product of their labour; they do not share in the company's profits which are secured by keeping their wages down and their productivity up. Yet they retain a direct interest in the firm's survival and prosperity, as employers never fail to remind them. Co-operation to this end cannot eliminate the antagonism built into the capital-labour relationship, but it does provide a counterbalance to it. Marxists have generally highlighted the conflicted nature of this relationship while ignoring or downplaying the conjoint interest of the classes. It follows from a more balanced appreciation of the labour-capital relationship that the parties have rational reasons both to fight and to co-operate with one another. We cannot say, *a priori*, which will predominate.

In the mid 1980s, it appeared to Dave, the union radical, that Stelco management was becoming much more responsive to worker interests:

> The entire attitude of the steel company has changed radically in the last two or three years, since we re losing money by the bucketful. You see the big companies that are closing down and you realize that Stelco could go bankrupt.... They're becoming more and more receptive to things now. Management has changed radically in the past few years.... Stelco is beginning to move toward a Volvo type model. I think the light has dawned very rapidly since the customers dried up, that if you want a good product, you want people to buy it, then the people who make it have got to do a good job, and you can't horsewhip anyone into doing a good job. They have to do it because they want to. But I think actually what is need is beginning to happen. (Dave, 1984)

A decade later, after closely observing the management changes related to worker participation measures, Dave concluded that:

> It's sadder looking at it now because of the deterioration. There's kind of like a hopeless feeling in a lot of the parts of the plant, it's just that nothing's working. In general, the management group is putting the program in place and the working group is producing the steel, and there s no communication there.... Computerized controls are getting rid of an awful lot of people on the plant floor. There's all kinds of jobs that used to be that don't exist anymore. But the management group is still just about as fat as before. The consultation process worked for a while. Then all this stuff dried up because they were tightening the budget and this was a really easy place to tighten. But when you stop communicating with the people on the plant floor who are doing the manufacturing, you stop the quality process. (Dave, 1994)

Conversely, Greg was indifferent to the union in 1984, but had strong feelings against having anything to do with management:

> These people that sit in offices down there, they shouldn't even be allowed out onto the job site, because all they are is office people. They are there only eight hours a day. They are not there at night time, after shift, or you know, where major things usually happen. To me they are useless. When they walk onto our job, everything comes to a standstill because they are over there trying to get this going and this going, and everybody just, just go away and leave us alone. Like the job was getting done when you weren't here. As soon as they walk onto the job, everybody just kind of scatters, because they don't want to hang around with them.... I don't even like talking to them. (Greg, 1984)

By 1994, in spite of his continuing criticism of arbitrary management practices, Greg's increased involvement in the union had convinced him of the need to try to co-operate with the company:

> Management still don't want to listen to us. We have asked for meetings on restructuring. Why don't you get a meeting together and listen to the guys' complaints and maybe it will help you out? It's just a farce, which is sad.... But I think you

are seeing a big change over, where the guys are starting to get more involved with the union because they see that it's reflecting on their job if they're not. I think the next contract [collective bargaining agreement] is going to be really crucial, worse than any of the others. But I honestly believe that the company and the union are working together now to get the job done. And that's what you need. (Greg, 1994)

While preserving the classical marxist thesis of endemic class conflict within profit-maximizing corporations (and public institutions facing sharp cuts), we question the assumption that the conflict between capital and labour will inevitably predominate over co-operation in the long run. The reality has been much more mixed.[37] Listening to Dave and Greg, we hear a complex amalgam of combative and co-operative responses to Stelco management's attempts to raise labour productivity.

Marxists have often been inclined to render a uniformly bleak view of manual wage labour, while underestimating or ignoring the interest and commitment many workers have in their work. The size of the paycheque is clearly a major factor but far from the whole story. Consider Dave's views of his job, one of the most responsible and highest paid ones in the steel plant:

Working with the introduction of new technology has been very interesting. Very interesting. It's really fun to learn, especially when you've been doing the same thing for some years.... As far as learning to operate this machine, you can't really put a date as to when you actually learn how to operate it. It's something that over the years you just acquire a feel for and then one night the operator doesn't show up and they'll say, okay, you're it now and that's when you start.... Anyone who takes a job on a machine that goes 24 hours a day, 7 days a week is not a playboy. You have picked a job mainly for the money.... I was one of the fortunate ones. I got in when things were good. I had never had a lay off. A few strikes, but it s been a pretty steady progression for me. So I can t complain. I m making pretty good money now and I have all along.... But I don't like the shifts, and the older I get, the harder the shifts get. I think the sooner I can get out of there, the better it will be for me. I'm hoping that when I get 30 years I can retire. (Dave, 1984)

Greg, on the other hand, had one of the dirtiest and poorest paid jobs in the plant in 1984, but he also was not completely alienated from his job:

> The heat is pretty bad but everyone gets along. You have to clown around because you have to work with each other eight hours a day. The work, anybody is capable of doing it. Male, female, handicapped, even.... This is the best place I ever worked down there. I don't want to leave. The front end has got a bad name. But they have cleaned it up now, a hell of a lot to what it used to be. It s fairly good down there, really. You run into chances to do other jobs that may be more skilled every day. You learn something different every day. (Greg, 1984)

Ten years later, he had a more skilled, higher paid job and sounded much like Dave had at about the same stage in his work life:

> I've got a lot of responsibility now and I'm getting fair compensation with raises and stuff like that, so I'm fairly satisfied. But I still work three shifts and it's getting a little rougher on me.... We're pretty near our own boss.... But they re pushing longer shifts and different training programs. They re striving and pushing the guys, the guys are upset about it, but they are coming around with good product. We've broken production records around here and the bosses are talking big bonuses.... Another ten years or so, all I have is another ten years to be eligible to get out of there, but I'll always be into some kind of work. (Greg, 1994)

The conservative consciousness of those subordinates who are more interested in "going along and getting along" than "rocking the boat" ought not to be treated as necessarily false, irrational or masochistic. [38] Subordinates are normally vulnerable to their superior's reprisals. They may reasonably seek to co-operate and avoid fights because they believe; a) that their compliance will be recognized and rewarded by their superiors; b) that the chance of producing beneficial change by fighting seems remote; or c) that gaining a victory at this time would probably trigger further rounds of mutually destructive recrimination which may put the enterprise at risk and; d) that the alternatives existing outside the relationship would be worse.

In order to understand the conservative responses of subordinates from a materialist perspective, we need to take seriously the joint nature of the enterprise (the firm or household, or even the community or the nation) which provides shelter and livelihood for both dominant and subordinate parties. Despite the stark disparities of effort and benefit, status and power, despite the conflicts generated on that account, subordinate members are dependent upon their bosses, househeads or political leaders for their livelihoods and well-being. Unless they are looking to leave in the short-term, they share an interest in preserving the unit as a thriving concern for as long as they remain personally dependent upon its continued existence and success to meet their own needs. For marxists, the personal insecurity of proletarian life under capitalism provides a compelling rationale for its overthrow; for workers, it has normally been a reason for pragmatic compliance.

A subtle mixture of combative and co-operative impulses has long been evident among Stelco workers. At the same time as they are resolved to fight for their rights if treated unfairly, they also worry about a deterioration in their relationship with management which might lower the company's productivity and frighten Stelco's customers, thus jeopardizing the company s prospects and the security of their own livelihood. Dave's criticisms of Stelco in 1984, for example, were focussed primarily on how mismanagement threatened the viability of the company:

> Stelco is very badly mismanaged, in that empires have been built. A boss at a high level must have a team that works under him that he can delegate his failures to. Each boss lower and lower down builds his own defence system until, well, we talk about this quite often, the fact that the company is so over-managed it's incredible. They're thinning it out now. This new works manager is not only being extremely cruel to us, he's also being cruel to management right now. So the over-management problem may cease to exist soon. But when we were making a lot of money, we were fat. These little empires were

built and the company was very poorly managed. There was the feeling that you could dictate to customers and they would just take whatever they were given. (Dave, 1984)

Ten years later, Greg strongly expressed similar criticisms of management, coupled with even more explicit allegiance to the company as his investment :

I hate work refusal down there which I've done quite a bit. That seems to be the only way you're going to get things fixed. I don t understand how a company can work that way.... They build a new facility and then they want to run it like a piece of junk. No way. I m sorry, that's my money sitting in there. That's your investment, my investment, and let's run it properly, the way it's designed to run. It just doesn't make sense to me, not when I'm involved in that partial investment. (Greg, 1994)

Within a broader universe of class relations, the bosses and workers in a given firm construct an ongoing dialogue based upon considerable knowledge of one another. If their conjoint enterprise is to be productive and enduring, it requires discussion between the parties, knowledge of the other s views (while holding one's own), awareness of how the other party is likely to respond to one's actions under a variety of circumstances.

Most Hilton steelworkers consider Stelco managers to be poor communicators: habitually secretive, they keep their own plans for the company s future to themselves, or present very selective versions to the workers; they have often misrepresented the company s financial position in contract bargaining; they cook up reorganization plans for the plant without consulting workers, then come down from on high at the last moment and expect to get instantaneous co-operation. Yet threats and bluffs, fights and intimidation, do not preclude negotiation, give and take, even mutual consideration and a degree of empathy, at times. If simmering hostilities are not to boil over and become mutually destructive, then cooler heads need to prevail on both sides. Explicit deals are hammered out and implicit understandings arrived at which serve to stabilize the relationship and subdue conflict for a time. When the pattern of past contractual agreements breaks down, however; when one party perceives that the deal we had with the other side has been unilaterally revoked, feelings of betrayal run high. From the workers' standpoint, the history of their relationship with Stelco management is strewn with the latter's broken promises.

Recognizing the deleterious impact on the bottom line of an acrimonious, distrustful relationship with their employees, Stelco managers periodically try to "turn the page," trumpeting a new era of co-operation and improved communication. While workers, with long memories, are often sceptical when managers talk in these terms, they nonetheless hope for a more co-operative and productive relationship. While taking place in a very different context, relations between domestic partners often manifest a similar character, as we will illustrate later.

Coming to an understanding with one another involves sharing a common language, filling in a world of common reference, exchanging opinions and perceptions. This is true whether we are considering collective bargaining at Stelco, ongoing negotiations between spouses concerning domestic responsibilities, or political deal-making in parliament. The consciousness of interdependent parties, particularly if they stay together for a long time, is bound to influence one another deeply. The more intimate the relationship, the more profound this intermingling of opinion and perspective is likely to be. Both conflict and co-operation shape consciousness. Power disparities do not make cultural conditioning unilateral, though they frequently make the influence of the subordinate party upon their common culture more difficult to discern and harder still to acknowledge publicly.[39]

Dominant partners pursuing their own interests are more likely to provoke the resistance of subordinates when they overturn implicit contracts and reduce the rewards for co-operating. The recent upturn in strikes in Canada seems to reflect these conditions. Despite the fact that corporate profits and executive pay have been rising rapidly for several years, workers have not received their traditional share of their firms prosperity via real wage increases. Co-operation is primarily being sustained by the threat of unemployment without the usual blend of positive incentives. Reducing the prospective rewards of co-operation diminishes the likelihood of continued labour peace. Even workers who are not predisposed to labour militancy may reluctantly conclude that they have no alternative but to fight back in order to defend their interests.

Certainly many unionized workers have a deep sense that co-operation with employers has clear limits which require collective organization to avoid being played off against other workers. As Greg puts it:

> I help out a lot of people that are in non-union shops with the knowledge that I got out of the union. They've got no representation or anything.... I have seen too many non-union shops and what guys are going through in there. It s either do this or you ain t got a job. I mean if they're telling me I got to do something unsafe, there is just no way. The contract, it's like a Bible, eh? (Greg, 1994)

Dave's comparative experience since retiring from Stelco has made him even more conscious of the need for worker solidarity against management:

> The companies I've been working with since Stelco are largely non-union, smaller businesses. The owners have complete control. As I watch the way they run the operations, they don't care about the welfare of their employees.... I guess with the recession and hard times you begin to think maybe workers are asking for too much. Then you go and see the reverse, you see what could be and that these people just work for themselves, a little core group of owners and managers. And the way they treat themselves, it just blows my mind the way these people take care of themselves, and the way they don't take care of their employees. It's the attitude in all these companies that, well, you know times are tough and if you don't like it, there's the door. And it will be for a long time because they know that for everyone that leaves there's a hundred and fifty that will come in the door. That's sad and it's frightening. (Dave, 1994)

The general image of class structure that is implicit in many of the above quotes is a tripartite one: an affluent group of owners and managers on top; regular wage earners and others who work for a living and have been able to get by in the middle; and the poor unemployed - Dave's hundred and fifty - on the bottom. Particularly in North America, the amalgamation of working- and middle-class is commonplace. Most working-class people see themselves in the middle of such a class structure, situated between the rich and the poor, but with a greater sense of social differences between themselves and the rich. Our two couples were representative of the Hamilton working-class in this respect in 1984:

> I'm middle income. I definitely think I'm part of a class system. Anyone who feels that this is an equal opportunity country is sadly mistaken. I believe anyone who thinks that a son of a doctor has the same things to look forward to as my son is a fool. If you're a steelworker, unless your son is brilliant, or your daughter, and gets a scholarship on merit, she's going to the school you can afford to send her. She's going to meet the people she can afford to meet. Rank has privilege, there's no doubt about it.... It infuriates me, my children are honours students, but if they want more than I have, they have very limited means of getting it. (Dave, 1984)

> I would say I'm middle class myself, because, as far as I am concerned, anybody that is right high class, I would just not even look at them, because they are snobs to begin with. They treat the working man like dirt, whether they knew you or not, the majority of them. The lower class people, I get along great with them. Like, I know a lot of people that are down in that bracket. (Greg, 1984)

> I would say we used to be lower class. The difference is income plus what people have got to show for it. I can only afford so much but now I've got what I want, my home, I have got kids and a car. We have no savings by any means, but what we do have is ours.... I've worked for a lot of high class people and most of the wives come out and say do you need any help? A lot of them were snobs. But most of them are down to earth people. Most of them had to work their way up there (Gilda, 1984)

A decade later, both couples continue to locate themselves in the middle of the class structure as they envision it. But their awareness of their own relative economic comfort and preoccupation with the growing class insecurity of both the burgeoning poor and their own children has increased considerably:

> There seems to be more of a class structure now. There was a gradual thing between the working-class and the white collar class. But I think there is now a very, very large part of the population that are poor. Whether it be working poor or just poor, there is a very large part of the population that probably live beyond my ability to understand how they are managing. We've always been comfortable, middle-class in the sense that we are making enough money that we are comfortable, able to cope. I ve always had good money. But we look at mostly young people that our kids know and you just can't fathom how they are managing. I see bitterness in that they don't have the opportunities that we had as a generation, and whether it leads to conflict or not, I don't know. (Dave 1994)

> I think the middle-class is being erased and it's mostly for the economy. I think your middle-class is becoming your poor. A lot of them have lost their jobs and are on welfare, like there are so many of them that had jobs like Dave. Those are gone, they are on welfare or whatever. They are becoming the poor. They are becoming really poor. I don't know what has happened. (Donna, 1994)

> I would say most of us working at Stelco are middle-class, simply because we're making a decent wage down there now. We got a little bit of security and pretty near everybody down there is either involved in a mortgage or owning their own home, stuff like that. So I would say it's middle-class. You look back and ask how we could have survived on them kind of wages. It's making a little bit more sense now with the money we're making and how we're surviving. It's changing...I know that I am one of the fortunate few. (Greg, 1994)

As mentioned, the fear of falling has become pervasive among people in both intermediate and working-class locations (cf. Newman, 1988; Ehrenreich. 1989; Rubin, 1994). With the intensification of competition between transnational firms, accelerated technological change and corporate downsizing, the primary labour market of secure jobs has shrunk drastically in advanced capitalist countries; the average duration of employment has shortened since the 1970s and traffic back and forth between the various ranks of employed and unemployed has increased greatly. In the wake of mass layoffs, this job insecurity was already widespread among workers who remained in the steel industry in the mid 1980s:

> I consciously think on a regular basis of what I would do when they say we're transferring your job and you won't be required, because I think it will happen.... Yes, I think about it. My kids are coming up to college soon and I do think about it. Like I don't know where I would go. I don't have a skill other than in the steel company. (Dave, 1984)

> They have eliminated jobs right, left and centre, because they get a machine to do that now. They figure, well, we are paying four guys to do this job a week, whereas if we spend this amount of money on this machine, put it in there and it will do the job for these guys. They are trying to advance too fast now, I think. The next tech change could take another 800 jobs. And that could be me, too, in ten years. The unemployment line. (Greg, 1984)

Ten years later, Greg was still in the steel plant with a better job, but his sense of insecurity had continued to grow:

> With the restructuring program, we re moving all over down there. Ninety-nine percent of us are just totally fed up with this restructuring. We understand that the company has got to do something. But the way it's being done and shoved down our throats, it s just criminal. And now there's going to be another big change. This is going to be happening and that, another restructuring program kicking right in. Like, senior men who've been doing a job for 35 years, washed right out, have to either retrain or be reduced to a simple labour job. I've only got half that seniority, what's going to happen to me? (Greg, 1994)

Race and Ethnic Consciousness

A major impact of recent economic restructuring on the group consciousness of the core of the employed working-class has been to make them both more aware of, and threatened by, the marginalized. Since visible minorities are more likely to be part of the reserve army of labour than whites are, members of the white working-class may tend to conflate minority status with economic marginality, while unemployed whites often blame employed minorities for taking their jobs. Above and beyond the competitive antagonisms fostered in the labour market, racial and ethnic conflict have been enduringly etched in group consciousness. Ethno-linguistic diversity is greater in Canada than in virtually any other advanced capitalist society. In recent years, the seemingly endless threat of Quebec's separation, the demands of native bands to settle land claims and concede self-government, have rubbed raw the sensibilities of many white people from the "rest of Canada." The strain of these larger national struggles has clearly dovetailed with local controversies over French schools, refugee claimants, police-minority relations, and so on. Against a backdrop of continuing high unemployment, these unresolved conflicts furnish ideal conditions for fomenting ethnic consciousness, racial suspicion, and a general lack of empathy between groups.

Most Hamilton steelworkers and their spouses are of British heritage. In common with others in this dominant ethnic group, they have tended to identify themselves as "just Canadian;" they take their cultural heritage for granted as the Canadian way of life. As tough times have persisted, they have become increasingly likely to perceive challenges to their established rights and identities from visible minorities. Affirmative action policies in hiring and crime rates in inner city neighbourhoods where minorities (and unemployment) have been more concentrated are key issues from their standpoint. Many in the white working-class now see such conflicts not only as the most evident but also as the most important conflict between groups in Canadian society.

Our two couples are generally progressive on both labour and civil rights issues. They continue to oppose racial discrimination. But as they have become increasingly concerned about their own families security and anxious about the potential impact of affirmative action policies upon the traditional advantages they have enjoyed in the labour market, they are now less empathetic to recent immigrants and visible minorities.[40]

Donna sees racial conflict primarily in terms of favouring minorities for secure jobs, while her well-qualified son and his white friends remain seriously underemployed. But clearly she is wrestling with the issues, and her position shifts slightly in the course of the following reflection:

> Somewhere somebody has to start standing up for the non-minority. We're becoming extinct, we have no rights anymore. Like look at my son, he couldn't get a job if he tried in the police force. It's no longer your ability, your education or whatever, it s your colour, and that's not right. That's not right. The people that are getting jobs haven't been held back, they're barely off the boat. They haven't been discriminated against. Half of them haven't earned the right to get a job. I don t know, maybe that s racist, I don't know. It's not nice to say but they're actually making you racist. They really are, because they are just throwing it down your throat, and they can t do that. Everybody should be equal and that means everybody. You should get it on your merit, not because of what you are. It's a delicate issue and I understand their side, too, you know. But let's be fair. I think the discrimination is making kids my son's age really angry. They really are. I mean it's not their fault what their great-great grandfathers did, you know what I mean?.... If there wasn't the unemployment you wouldn't have the anger. You wouldn't have the problem. But with the unemployment, it's making these kids very angry. And I can understand it, but you have to have equality, too. There was discrimination against the minority, always has been and that's not right.... But I think maybe the problem is being solved too quickly. Maybe the quotas are too high. If a minority went for a job and he was better than the white person, he should get it. Whether he did or not, I don't know.

> That's the problem. But right now, with my son's generation paying for it, it's really not fair. (Donna, 1994)

Dave expresses similar concerns about reverse job discrimination against his son and his friends. Although he declares shock at the strength of their racist views, he constructs a clear opposition between my country and "other people:"

> My son and a lot of his friends have very, very red-neck tendencies. These kids are well educated, but there's a bitterness. You know, a fellow is working at a pizza place and can't get another job because somebody has quotas that they have to have. When they are all here and a lot of his friends say things, it s frightening. But it's a way they perceive things because they go out looking for jobs and there are a lot of doors closed that are open to other people.... I have some strong feelings about Canada as a melting pot and I agree probably with one thing that happens in the United States that I don't see here. If you come to my country, you are more than welcome to become part of my country. But don' t come to my country and set down rules that say I came here but I will still have this and this and this legislated as being my right because it was brought here from another country. I don't know if I m right or wrong. It's my answer. (Dave, 1994)

Gilda's kids are still in school and she is trying hard to raise them to be racially tolerant. But she makes a similar polarity to Dave in her interpretation of ethnic struggles, between "one Canadian way" under siege and hate-prone foreign-born minorities:

> I think that Canadians are becoming a minority. [Governments] are trying so hard to make it right for everybody that they are going to screw up big time, sooner or later. People came to Canada to get away from what they are and what they were in and they are trying to change it to what they had. But you can't do that. You come to Canada for freedom for what you believed in, and to get away from what you had, yet they bring it with them. They bring the hate with them, they bring the violence with them. I think the policy should be if you are leaving for violence and hate and coming to Canada to be-

come a Canadian, then everybody has to learn to work with everybody as one, as a whole country. It can't be his way or her way. I think we are trying too hard to change it to suit everybody and you can't. It's got to stay one way and everybody falls into that. I think they are trying too hard with minorities and there is too much racism calls over little things. I think that if people stopped complaining about little things, the bigger things would look after themselves.... I think that racism starts in the home. If it stops there, it's not going to go any place. That's what I teach my children. They are the same as you inside, there is no difference. (Gilda, 1994)

Greg also espouses strong wishes to end the racial prejudice and ethnic conflicts which he sees as rampant in Canada. But, while he recognizes that unemployment and crime rates are highly correlated, he tends to think of criminal behaviour in them and us terms: the law-abiding established white groups of this free country versus the minorities who are prone to crime waves :

There is no racial prejudice in my home. But in Hamilton, it's tough for people in a lot of neighbourhoods. I keep an eye on that stuff in my community work. If you get a high crime area, it's usually the unemployed that are heavily involved in the crime.... There are big changes because you re finding ethnic groups running, you know, like their festivals and that a lot more. The biggest conflict right now is the Croatians and the Serbians because of what's going on in their homeland. I see it at work every day. Now guys are just starting to put that aside. But then you look at the crime statistics and who is doing them. You know, you got minorities that are involved in a lot of the crime waves that are going on. That's where I feel that the government should be doing something. You're a brother and you come over to this country to live in a free country. Man, abide by the laws, that's all I want you to do. You want to break them, then why should they be put in jail here? Why should you and I have to pay? Send them back to where they came from. That's my view on it.... I'd like to get rid of the prejudice of the Canadian people. Canadian people are very prejudiced. You know, with the French going on with what's happening in Quebec now. But that's the way things are going, that's the way it's going to happen. I'm only one person. (Greg, 1994)

This is not the virulent racism of the Heritage Front type, based in notions of inherent white superiority. But it reflects a growing fear that a way of life which these families have struggled to attain, based upon the lifetime security of the male breadwinner s wage, is now jeopardized. Donna articulates the nature of this fearful and uncertain group consciousness, while trying to reconcile it with anti-racist principles:

We don't use downtown Hamilton anymore. It's dirty. There are too many gangs. I wouldn't walk through central square if you paid me.... Hamilton now has a lot of racial problems that it never had either. The racial conflict. I don t care how many races there is, it doesn t matter. But, like in the high schools you've got Portuguese against Chinese, and there are so many gangs in the schools. Even at the parks down here it's just like gangs everywhere. It's terrible, it never used to be like that. There was always a multitude of kids in the schools; they weren't all white, you know. But there didn't seem to be a problem. Maybe it's just the way we perceive things. But I think Hamilton is more threatening now, a lot more threatening. I don't think it matters where you go. You go out at night for a walk or whatever, and there's kids, gangs, everywhere, everywhere. I don't know. (Donna, 1994)

The social distance between these members of the white working-class and visible minorities is palpable. While both couples express support for principles of racial equality, they convey little sense of familiarity or empathy with the conditions faced by those with darker faces due to racial discrimination. There are a few Hamilton steelworkers in inter-racial marriages and others active in the local anti-racist movement. But, for the most part, the white working-class scarcely knows these potential allies who share their interest in overcoming social inequality. In the context of diminishing material prospects, particularly for their children, they are inclined to blame those beneath them in the class structure, and governments who seem to be bending over backwards to assist them, for the increased vulnerabilities of their own, caught-in-the-middle class.[41]

Gender Consciousness

As the labour force participation rates of married women have risen in the past three decades, and the feminist movement has pushed for a fuller recognition of women's employment rights, men who were generally progressive have tended to support women's right to equal access and equal pay both in principle and for their own wives. Dave and Greg expressed support for women steel workers in 1984, in the aftermath of the Women Back into Stelco campaign:

> It's perfectly natural. My wife has worked in a factory. I had a woman on my crew. I don't think she made any difference.... I think it's natural. I think what we've done in the past 40 years is unnatural, in the fact that it was an all-male environment. Steelmaking is not, doesn't require a great amount of brawn. It's pretty well a push-button business now. (Dave, 1984)

> I have worked with women in the past. Some of them were better workers than the guys down there. Some guys would help out the nice looking girls. I don't buy that routine. If they are making the same money I am, they are going to do the same job I am going to do. They're capable of doing the same job. The majority of the work down there, anybody is capable of doing it. (Greg, 1984)

However, as jobs continued to become scarcer and younger women perceptibly more assertive, both men became more uncomfortable in their everyday relations with women workers and more circumspect in their support for gender equity in the work place:

> In the old days, the "good old boys" were running places like the steel mill. That male preserve deal had to change. Maybe we were particularly lucky but women came into our department and they blended in, there wasn t a problem with them at all. You heard about the isolated incident, the kind of thing

> that gets into the newspaper, but what I saw was that people came into the plant and wanted to work just because the money was good and the work was there. We had no problems whatsoever.... But what I see happening now terrifies me. I worked for years with women and felt completely comfortable. But now I find that a lot of things, like sexual discrimination and sexual harassment and things of this nature are working to the detriment of men. I don t know how to explain it. I don t feel comfortable working with a woman now because I feel threatened. Now I constantly have to think if I m doing anything that is wrong or can be perceived as harassment of any sort. I feel very, very threatened now working with a woman. (Dave, 1994)

> To me, if you are capable of doing the job, it's yours. I don't like the idea of this quota hiring of women. I'm against that, especially in certain areas, not only in the steel making industry. Really, it wouldn't matter too much down there. It would in the police department, fire department. Your necessary jobs outside of what I do, no - I don't agree with quota hiring. I feel it should be on their merit, their knowledge, everything.... I think there's starting to get a lot of conflict in relations between men and women now. I think that they are trying to outdo one another. Because you have women's groups coming up and they have got to have a strong voice in this country, whether people realize it or not. I mean, that way I think they are trying to push apart from the male. And in other ways, it's working. Because some males, like myself, I don't care. If a woman's got a view, she could be right on it. I'm not saying that she always is. There are some views these women's groups got that I just totally disagree with. But, you know, the majority speaks, I got to put up with it.... I mean if we all work at it, we can all be just as good as each other. It's the way I look at people. I don't look at men or women, I look at people. (Greg, 1994)

While the male-breadwinner family ideal is not nearly as compelling as it was in its heyday, the financial power of the male paycheck persists. Even in dual-earner households, men's income normally exceeds their spouses; the latter's economic dependency remains considerable. In our sample, employed wives earned, on average, just 38% of the annual income of their husbands (well below the Canadian average), while doing about twice the amount of housework and meal preparation. Many commentators assume that, with the rise of feminism and the shift to a two-earner norm, Canadian society has virtually achieved, or is well on its way to attaining, equality between the sexes. While some progress has undoubtedly been made in the past thirty years, we are more sanguine. As long as most women are paid much less than men, while doing much more unpaid family work than their partners do, then the twin pillars of conjugal inequality will persist, anchoring gender inequality in all spheres.

Wives and husbands inhabit different social positions within the household and have, in consequence, very different experiences of domestic life. But they do not live in separate worlds. They speak the same language, but talk differently; they view the same situation, but see it differently; both are active in maintaining the household, but with different roles and prerogatives. In all likelihood, in today's society they both watch television and read newspapers, while selecting their preferred programs and articles differently; so they are subject to different snippets of the commercially promulgated news discourse of the day. Both observe the unfolding drama of the world outside the home, but do so from distinct vantage points, with different opportunities for participation in it. But much like the relationship between managers and workers, and with much greater intimacy, the longer they stay together and the more economically interdependent they become, the more their views of gender relations converge. In 1984, Donna expressed concern about sexual harassment of younger women in her work place. By 1994, her discomfort with feminist demands and the changing sensibilities in gender relations was at least as great as her husband's:

> I think the women's movement has gotten totally out of hand.... When the government says you have to have x number of women, x number of men, why? It should be every-

body that is a hundred percent qualified. If the woman is not as qualified as the man that applies, why should she get the job because she is a woman? All you are doing is meeting your quota and you are covered and that's not right. I don't think it is anyway. I really don t think it s right. Like, as a woman myself, I wouldn't want to get the job knowing that I got it because I'm a woman. I want it because I'm good.... I think they just dislike men. I really do. I think they look on the men as the enemy instead of just the person. I really do. And I think that it's stupid, stupid. I ve worked with men and women and there was never a problem. You just worked as co-workers and there was no problem. Like my boss will come out and put his arm on my shoulder and lean over to do something, but he won't do that with the younger woman in the office because that's a no-no. Like, what's the big deal? It's far too serious and it's totally different.... See, I missed it. It just baffles my mind. I don't understand these feelings. (Donna, 1994)

Donna's lack of empathy for younger women indicates, once again, the difficulty of any theoretical perspective that derives group consciousness simply from having a social location within that group. Consciousness of class, race and gender identities and interests is a process of continual interaction. Those who are caught in the middle may be intensely critical of elites, but as they become more insecure, they are increasingly pre-occupied with perceived threats from below.

Note the similarity between the arguments of our respondents on race and gender issues. They are against reverse discrimination, against movements of the oppressed that have gone too far. In rejecting affirmative action arguments for collective advancement, they have fallen back on a market rationale (to be discussed more fully below) where everyone competes *as individuals* for scarce resources, and people ought to be hired strictly on their merits *regardless* of their race or sex (i.e. without regard to pre-existing conditions of inequality). Our respondents have not adopted this abstract individualism, so prevalent in public discourse, because white working-class people cannot think for themselves or have fallen under the sway of alien class ideas. They have taken up a market rationale because it is well-suited to the defence of their interests as they construe them along race, gender, and class-sectional lines. Most white working-class people are adopting forms of group consciousness that support their race and gender privileges (including a defence, by many women, of the labour market prerogatives of the men they live with). In the face of dwindling jobs and strong feminist and anti-racist challenges to the *status quo*, support for social equity, still upheld in principle, becomes increasingly difficult to reconcile with the maintenance of personal security as global competitiveness hits home.

We find the repudiation of affirmative action regrettable, but also understandable. It is certainly not irrational or contrary to their (one) true interest. A more inclusive and powerful working-class movement could generate an alternative axis of solidarity and collective uplift that would provide these people with another way to align their interests. Our principal regret is that such an alternative does not now exist.

The Inter-Generational Impasse

For the families at the core of the Hamilton working-class, the avenues of labour force renewal that were present in the steel industry throughout the post-war boom have been shut down entirely since the recession of the early 1980's. Almost no youths have been hired on at Hilton Works since then; by 1996, less than one-half of 1% of the plant's entire work force was less than 35 years old, while the average age had risen to 47. This particular labour force is not renewing itself at all! The blockage is a severe instance of the general labour-force bottleneck, where youth are having to stay in school longer (or return to school after failing to find work) while their entry into full-time year-round employment is delayed until they are well into their twenties. By 1994, only 42% of Canadians aged15-24 were in the labour force.[42] Despite the fact that the size of the youth cohort seeking entry is small compared with the baby-boom generation immediately ahead of it, youth unemployment remains very high, almost twice the national average. With labour force renewal bogged down, nuclear-family turnover is prolonged as well. In the post-war boom, most young people found a mate, left home and set up their own households by their early twenties. Now, at that age, they are much more likely to be living at home, unable to find steady work.

> I don't think there's going to be as many jobs for them as there was when we were going out....I know a lot of people that I worked with are students... I was married at 21; these people are 23 and 24 and they don't own a home, they're still living with their mom and dad whereas I wasn't; I was working from the time I was 16 on.... When I got out of grade 12, it seemed like there was a lot available. You could apply to Bell Canada; you could apply anywhere. Whereas the students now, it seems to me it's more they have to know somebody or be there at the right time.... 23, 24 - they're not really kids anymore....They re disillusioned... They don't know what to do with themselves... These people are making the lowest wage you can make.... I don't like what I see. Hopefully, things will have improved by the time my kids are at that stage in the game, because I don't know if I'd want the kids here when they're 24, 25....You know, that's a scary situation, because at that age, you're an adult. [1994, Female, ID# 78]

The acceleration of technological change and economic restructuring, the rapidity with which occupational niches are overrun and jobs are devoured by computer-based machinery, has discouraged longer-term career-planning. Young working-class men in Hamilton today have a far more difficult time finding good jobs than did their elders; very few can expect to succeed by following the employment strategies their fathers used.

> For the younger people just starting off, I think it's going to be really difficult. You pick a trade or something you want to get into and then, by the time you get there, it's too many people or there's not enough jobs. When I grew up, there was always the Stelcos and the Dofascos and the Harvesters and there was always jobs there, you know.... I had grade 12... I went back to school for two weeks in grade 13 and said, no, I'm working. But the jobs were there. I mean, if you didn't like this job, you could go to another job. It seemed like after '81 things changed dramatically, and people still out of work aren't find-

> ing jobs or working here and there or whatever.... I think right until 1980, things were all right. But after that, things are just changing. Seems like every time you get the paper, somebody's closing down and technology has taken a huge bite out of it, no doubt about it. But, I don't know. It s going to be hard for the kids. You keep telling them to get an education but the jobs aren't there. It's not going to help. [1994, Male, ID # 140]

A growing body of comparative empirical research has documented that the current generation of youth in advanced capitalist societies brings unprecedented levels of educational qualifications to the labour market, but also has experienced unprecedented levels of underemployment of their knowledge and skill. Canadians are spending significantly more time in schooling, further adult education courses and informal learning on their own than in prior generations. However, structural unemployment, involuntary temporary employment in poor jobs, overqualification for the actual performance requirements of available jobs and a subjective sense of being underemployed have all increased significantly over the past 20 years (see Livingstone, 1999). A young black woman with a college degree, now working as a room attendant, put it this way:

> Whenever I look at my paycheck I feel down and low. And I know I might be stranded here forever.... I feel embarrassed to tell others what I do for a living. Whenever I say I'm a room attendant, others will lose their interest in me and say "oh." That's the end of the conversation.... It's not only about the money. I feel mentally and physically exhausted after cleaning sixteen rooms a day in a motel. It's a very stressful experience. You feel you're worthless after all the education and hard work you put in to better yourself. It's rough. (Livingstone, 1999, p. 105).

While some of those who remain in the old core of the Hamilton working-class still feel relatively secure in their own jobs, neither they nor their children see much prospect that the younger generation will achieve a comparable level of job security in their lifetimes.

The Critical Insights of Subordinated Viewpoints

Subordinates' more critical views typically remain hidden from their superiors. Safe havens for their most candid thoughts are usually rare, and not only on class grounds.[43] Our research was conducted in workers homes with the endorsement of a strong militant trade union, a commitment to give back the findings to the workers, and generally warm rapport with our respondents. We would not expect workers to freely express their more critical views on class relations with their bosses present. In gender terms, there were similar constraints. Male breadwinner power still prevails in most steelworkers households. Interviewed alone by another woman in 1984, Donna talked freely about sexual harassment in her work place. In 1994, when she was interviewed together with Dave and by a male interviewer, Donna offered the more anti-feminist views quoted above and spoke profusely about her concerns for her son s future but little about her daughter s. Gilda remained largely silent on gender issues and displayed some tensions with her husband over their different interests in community activities when they were interviewed together. The critical insights of visible minorities remain entirely beyond the scope of these interviews conducted by and with all-white participants. Nevertheless, we suggest that gender and racial subordination are likely to generate analogous insights to those discussed here in terms of class subordination.

Marx argued that, whilst harnessed to the accelerated rhythms of machinery and driven to exhaustion by bosses striving to squeeze more surplus value from their labour, workers were privileged in one crucial respect. Toiling at the heart of capitalist enterprise, they had a special epistemological vantage point. Divorced from productive property, alienated from the capital they set in motion, they were able to see through market-based claims of equal opportunity, and could instead appreciate the fundamental reason for capitalist inequality, based upon the appropriation of their labour in the "hidden abode" of production.[44] Furthermore, production workers were in a unique position to offer the broad ranks of the labouring classes a counter-ideology of socialist co-operation which expressed their own collective interests, but also held out the promise of a broader, more universal, emancipation. What aspects of this hypothesis can be maintained and applied as a general proposition to those occupying subordinated positions in work places, in the family economy, and in racially stratified cities?

We think it is generally true that people who are disadvantaged by prevailing arrangements are less inclined to actively defend the status quo, more likely to see the basic unfairness of the system and to resent its inequities. This tendency applies to visible minorities and women as much as to the working-class. The oppressed may believe in a society's promoted ideals with just as much fervour as the privileged, but they are more likely to be sceptical concerning its capacity to measure up to espoused ideals, having suffered the gap between rhetoric and reality first-hand. The rapidity with which mass consciousness can change in moments of upheaval confirms that people's compliance during quiescent periods is more likely to be obtained through the "dull compulsions of everyday life" than by means of a firm belief in the basic justice of the existing social order.

Against the flattening out of postmodernist theory, where all social relations are thought of as "text," we want to retain the marxist insight concerning the layered, opaque and deceptive nature of capitalist social relations, where free and fair exchange in the marketplace conceals and misrepresents the social relations of production within firms and households. The genesis of bourgeois ideology lies in the misleading appearance of commodity relations, not in capital s control of the press (Marx, 1967). In the marxist conception, percept comes before concept, the magic of the free market before the propagation of bourgeois ideas. As Fredric Jameson (1991) has remarked: "The ideological dimension is intrinsically embedded within reality, which secretes it as a necessary feature of its own structure." (p. 262).

The cornerstone of bourgeois ideology is an optic that places capitalism in the best possible light by leaving the rest of society beyond the market in the shade. The rationale of fair exchange is that people come to the market with their eyes open. Since everyone is free to turn down an offer they don t like, and no self-interested person would make a deal that is not of benefit to themselves, free market transactions can only proceed on the basis of mutual benefit. Dissatisfied with the result? Market contracts are short-term and can be readily terminated by either party, so if people feel they are getting a raw deal, they can take their business elsewhere. Would free and intelligent people repeatedly engage in transactions which exploited them? Of course not. While any particular transaction may turn out to be inequitable, a competitive market must foster free and fair exchange in the long run because self-interested parties will insist on it. Consequently, markets should be permitted to operate without interference because the state is not obliged to defend people who are free to defend themselves.

In this perspective, the key articles of faith in upholding capitalism's basic fairness are predicated upon an abstract notion of the equality of free individuals. Abstract, because liberal ideology refuses to consider pre-existing social inequalities in the rest of their lives, treating them as if they were naturally equals "*regardless* of sex and race" before setting foot in the marketplace. Hence, the supreme symbol of justice is blindfolded. No one can be faulted, or credited, for the fortune of their birth; yet the social location of children is the major determinant of their life-chances as adults. In spite of these huge initial disparities, the dominant interpretation of Western legal codes typically ties the hands of public institutions seeking to redress the imbalance by prohibiting them from treating people differently, making special provisions for the disadvantaged, because that preference is held to breach the principle of equality upon which the rule of law is based. Formal equality thus serves to buttress the reproduction of substantive inequality passed down from generation to generation. This is why feminists and anti-racists who seek to rectify historic disadvantages through policies of affirmative action can so easily be accused of "reverse discrimination" or "special treatment."

In a powerful insight, Marx recognized the close connection between Western legal principles of formal equality and contractual freedom, and the layered structure of capitalist society. In his words, the sphere of exchange was "the very Eden of the innate rights of man" (1967, p. 172). Stark inequalities of wealth and income are *realized* through market exchange, but they do not originate in those formally symmetrical transactions where buyers and sellers meet to conduct business, apparently on an equal footing. They have a prior basis in the asymmetric nature of the transactions between the owners of capital and labour-power in the hidden abode of production .[45] We can apply the same reasoning to the relations between men and women in the hidden abode of the household, which play no small part in the unequal values their labour power realizes when they sell it to employers. The result of both transactions, in combination, is private capital accumulation. Most people who own capital to begin with end up enriching themselves; almost all who lack capital to begin with spend wage-income in order to live and end up returning to work tomorrow to augment capital's value once again.

Marx recognized that workers were well placed to see through this game, where the above-board rules of the market-place seemed fair, but capital dealt cards, beneath the table, from a stacked deck. Their revelation would come in the form of the labour theory of value - not as scholarly treatise, but as an instinctive feeling of being "ripped off." [46] When class-conscious workers insist that " the bosses are getting rich off of our labour," when they perceive that the shareholders' profits ultimately derive from the firm's appropriation of the fruits of their labour, they have discovered a major wellspring of capitalism's inequality. To this day, many production workers glean this insight.

> There is a conflict between management people who are making a lot more money and we ain't getting nothing out of it. Now we're doing the work and slaving for you, why don't we get a cut? (Greg, 1994)

> I think the truest thing I ever heard has got to be many years ago now. A very, very knowledgeable skilled operator who was a very philosophical kind of a guy told me once that this company won't do anything unless they're guaranteed to make a profit. They never ever stick their necks out.... I'm very cyni-

cal about the suggestion plan. Over the years, the suggestion plan has been used to pay people who are very co-operative. If you're a good boy and you re very co-operative, the suggestion plan will pay you for almost nothing. And if you have a tendency to question things then you don't get paid for great suggestions. I've seen other people slighted terribly that have come up with amazing ideas. (Dave, 1984).

The free capitalist system is extremely popular right now. But to me it is extremely unfair because I think over a period of years that we are producing a complete society of haves and have nots. That's what I believe we are beginning to see now because of the "free market." (Dave, 1994)

Let's face it, things are going down hill. They are taking too much money out of the workers who need it and not enough out of the people who don't need it...and they don't put any of it back into the community. (Gilda, 1984)

By the same token, most working-class men greatly exaggerate the actual extent of recent changes in gender relations. The reality is that there are still very few women in steel plants, or in other well-paid male bastions such as executive office-suites, corporate boardrooms, or government cabinets. Women still receive lower pay for work of comparable value and are further burdened by a very inequitable division of labour at home which has changed only slightly as married women in increasing numbers have gone out to work. As Connell (1995, p. 240) rightly observes: "The general interest of men in patriarchy is formidable. It was badly underestimated by sex role reformers and it is easily underestimated still." But it is not downplayed by the working-class women we interviewed (Livingstone and Luxton, 1996, p. 129):

It's still male-dominated, it's not equal. I mean, we can fight for equal pay and stuff but it's still male-dominated. I don't think you will ever get away from it; I don't think you will ever see a society where it's equal, not really. It's improved from what it used to be where we had absolutely no rights. But even sexually, they're still dominant I think.

> Men are *starting* to realize that they can't just be the breadwinner and come home to a home-cooked meal and that's it. Women are working now and you can't do it that way. But there's still an awful lot of men that just don't want to change. Even my husband, he'll always say: "what is there to do?" And later on he'll say, "why didn t you tell me you had all that stuff to do?" Well, you can hear me doing the dishes, why don't you come in and help me? I hate to *ask* you to do everything. If I'm still working, you should still be working.

Subordinates do have a unique vantage point from which to observe the functioning of the organizations in which they toil. They come to know the operation of the capitalist work place, the patriarchal household, or the geography of a city's race relations, up close, in detail, and from below, looking up at the underbelly of the beast. They develop forms of knowledge and often unacknowledged skills that their bosses, house heads, or more affluent, white suburban neighbours, surveying the field from on high, do not possess. They are normally in the best position to observe discrepancies between rhetoric and reality. This accounts, in part, for the widespread disdain that shop floor workers have for front office managers; that women have for men's domestic expertise; that inner-city residents have for city planners; and "practical" working-class people have for academics "in their ivory towers." As Greg put it in 1984: "The company is coming out and saying, you know, we will save your jobs if you will do this. It's all brainwashing. That is part of their ploy."

When class subordination in production is coupled with strong collective organization, such as Stelco's militant union local, USWA 1005, oppositional thought is also more likely to identify economic and political alternatives to currently institutionalized structures. Both of our couples combine their skepticism of management's optimistic claims with support for more democratic and egalitarian forms:

> You could be looking at work-sharing projects as a means of getting people back to work. Changing scheduling, shorter work hours. It would mean a loss in wages. But I think, for the

> overall good, I think the average man would go to some sort of work-sharing program. In fact, it was discussed, I think, at a local plant and I think they actually did it. They went to work sharing where they worked four days a week, and for every four people that worked a four day week, it made one extra job. (Dave, 1984)

> There is no reason why Stelco shouldn't be hiring another thousand people. That's how short of people they are as far as I am concerned. They've got jobs down there that just aren t getting done because of the lack of manpower. And then there's the overtime on top of that. Bang, there's jobs sitting there waiting.... The economy would be a lot better. If people are working, they wouldn't be so disgruntled. People have to be busy. (Greg, 1994)

> I think the worker needs more say and more input and more control, even in investing the company's profits. (Donna, 1994)

> I really think we need something closer to democracy than what we have right now. I could go into a three hour diatribe. Something a little closer to democracy than the club system that Canada operates on right now, and the United States operates on it. It's a very closed network, club, that takes care of itself and doesn't really care that much about the average citizen. Power structures and lobbies, if you're in the right lobby group, you can get a lot of things done. (Dave, 1984)

The basic weakness of the subordinates' viewpoint is that it is typically local. Normally they are pinned down by the nature of their work and supervisory constraints; they find it difficult to move around and compare notes with their counterparts at other sites. Since they cannot directly observe the close parallels in their situation, a sub-strata of extensive social relations remain hidden from them. They need regular networks of horizontal communication to pool knowledge among themselves and develop a broader, more comprehensive analysis of the operation of the system-at-large. This is what inclusive industrial unions and grassroots civil rights movements were originally designed to do - to promote horizontal communication and solidarity. In their present forms, however, union and civil rights bureaucracies normally inhibit horizontal networking between locals and chapters in different cities, channelling communication vertically between the local unit and central headquarters.

Women's subordination is predicated, in part, upon their personal dependence upon particular men (fathers, boyfriends, spouses) and their competitive isolation from one another in the pursuit of these relationships. When feminists formed consciousness-raising groups in the 1970's, they found that many women were radicalized by the experience of confiding in one another, "breaking the silence" and discussing the remarkable similarities in their intimate partnerships with men. Here too, we discern the critical importance of horizontal communication between peers in similar but separate settings, spreading awareness of common conditions and ways of improving their lot.

The alienation of subordinates from the structures of power and persuasion does not readily lead to the formation of revolutionary consciousness, due in part to the limitations they face in developing and maintaining horizontal communication. The constraints of their positions make it particularly difficult for them to develop a counter-ideology, envision an effective concrete alternative, or map out a viable strategy for change.

Multiple Identities, the Integrated Self and Critical Thought

Whether conformists or rebels, we are creatively active in the construction of our views of the world and our responses to it. We do not, of course, develop our outlook on our own; we are culturally immersed in communities of shared meaning. But insofar as our social location is multiply determined and the rational pursuit of self-interest does not normally dictate a singular course of action, we have some leeway in how we interpret our circumstances and respond to them. Language is part and parcel of this subtle dialectic between constraint and choice. On the one hand, our language universe is inescapable and externally imposed. We are not free to determine the meanings we place upon words; if we are interested in communicating with others, we must accept this discipline. On the other hand, language is expressive. In speaking, we combine words in rule-governed ways, but nevertheless in ways that permit us to develop our own thoughts in the process of articulation.

In our view, most postmodernists treat language in an excessively determinist way, as a mental straightjacket rather than a communicative resource (Jameson, 1972). While underestimating the force of material circumstances, they have exaggerated the power of prevailing discourses to mould and effectively silence people in subordinated positions. While discourses certainly do construct subject positions ; the converse is also true; people construct discourses. They never do so *ex nihilo*; they remake existing discourses. When the expressive leeway of speakers is slighted, so too is the capacity of common people to develop distinct views and to speak their minds. Given the opportunity in our in-depth interviews to reflect upon their experience, our respondents did not simply repeat what they had heard experts say; they were often highly articulate and employed language expressively to develop their own distinct views and convey deeply personal meanings.[47]

Postmodernist theory offers a dystopia of omnipotent discourses constructing our innermost desires. Within this conception, the integral person is replaced by the decentred subject, ostensibly a more sophisticated notion.[48] This is devastating to any political perspective of subordinated peoples struggling self-consciously to end their oppression. Throughout the modern era, progressive social theorists have always held that subordinated people are not merely the bearers of pre-established social relations, but are capable of thinking critically about, and potentially transforming, those relations. Is there any reason to abandon this premiss beyond confirming a general pessimism with current prospects for progressive change? We will argue that there is plenty of convincing evidence to the contrary. Even in relatively settled periods, incipient resistance is common, both among individuals in relation to oppressive micro-contexts and among groups in relation to extensive structures of dominance.

It is important to be realistic about the capacity to remake the world from below. We are not simply oppressed by social structures laid on from above; we participate every day in their reproduction simply by carrying out the routines of daily life. This, more than ideological dominance, is what makes social order possible. Growing up, we come to recognize the social world as an external reality distinct from ourselves, as a set of arrangements that we can sometimes influence but do not control. We learn how the social institutions we inhabit work, the rules of the game in the various spheres of life, and what others expect of us. In conforming to their expectations, most of us are motivated by a strong need for approval. We also discover that breaking rules is often painful, that a modicum of law-abiding conformity is necessary simply to get along, just as, with the physical world, we learn to avoid walking into walls or over cliffs.[49] None of this precludes resistance.

Despite persistent pressures to conform in order to discharge the routines of daily life, people display the capacity to be critical of the ways their environment is structured. We can conform and dissent at the same time. We can get along at a level sufficient to sustain our place (keep our job, stay in school, remain at home) while resisting or evading those rules or conventions we find unfair. Furthermore, we are able to generalize from particular injustices to elaborate a larger critique.

All social movements bent upon changing the established order rely upon the human capacity for deliberate resistance in the midst of superficially conforming practice in order to launch their campaigns. For how else would dissent develop and individuals get together to create an organized opposition prior to open revolt? While large-scale resistance is necessarily collective, the capacity for resistance must be present in individuals.[50] Social theorists who slight people's desires for self-integration, such as those quoted below, propose a profoundly depoliticizing basis for collective action.

> Is it necessary to have a coherent identity? We think not. We often find ourselves with senses of ourselves that are in conflict without finding this a problem. The idea that a self must have a coherent identity is standard fare in the humanist tradition, that which supposes that identity is regulated by a coherent ego.[51]

No wonder that the authors, Kaufman and Marin, find (to cite the title of their article) a "chasm of the political" in postmodern theory. The postmodernist critique of abstract and ultra-rationalist models of the autonomous individual based upon idealized notions of the sovereign ego is well-taken. But we insist that most people (and certainly our Hamilton respondents) strive to integrate their various identities in all spheres of life; they make an ongoing effort to reconcile discordant impressions, minimize cognitive dissonance, balance impulse with restraint, avoid being two-faced, and behave consistently according to certain basic principles.[52] Few achieve complete integration; often, we have different senses of ourselves in various contexts. But most of us are not content to leave these facets unintegrated, to experience ourselves as fragmented, dissociated and incoherent.

In a more subtle commentary, Calhoun has written:

> throughout history and still to a considerable extent today we find multilingualism common; we find people moved simultaneously by different visions of the world (not least, religion and science); we find people able to understand themselves as members of very differently organized collectivities from families to communities, states or provinces, nations and international organizations, and to recognize themselves through different identities at different times and stages of life.[53]

It is true, of course, that people have several identities and move daily through milieu where they are required to embrace different styles of thought and speak in different discourses. The institutions and groups they belong to make different demands upon them, require them to behave differently and evince different priorities. This is the condition of modernity, exacerbated by quickening technological change and the frenetic pace of contemporary urban life. It may make some people's lives rich and diverse; more often, it creates stress, as people struggle to balance work and family, wrestling with disparate demands and divided loyalties. Television compounds the problem of fragmentation, as our senses are bombarded daily with disconnected 'sound bytes' and dazzling, often jumbled, visual images. There are undoubtedly increasing pressures towards a de-centered subjectivity in the world today. But does this make personal integrity an illusion?[54]

Through all the disparate spheres of life, most of us experience ourselves as one person: we answer to the same name, inhabit the same body, have a single brain which integrates our diverse experiences. In making sense of our lives, we impose coherence upon segmented experience and memory. Above all, we strive to reconcile our subjective dispositions with externally-imposed realities.

Postmodernists have correctly highlighted powerful disintegrative forces at work in the world today, stemming from the cultural logic of late capitalism.[55] Too often they seem to advise us to relax and enjoy the breakdown. We believe that resisting the centrifugal forces of contemporary culture is a realistic and ethical option for individuals and oppressed groups. Why disparage such efforts by dismissing the integral self as a naive delusion? We are opponents of individualism; but the individual, *per se*, is not an ideological construct of bourgeois society.[56] Resisting personal fragmentation is a profoundly healthy impulse. It is precisely because of this psychological work that common people who are not party to the latest intellectual trends do not doubt their singular personhood and generally equate mental wholeness with sanity.[57] More power to them!

In growing into adulthood, most people attain a core identity that stays with them throughout the rest of their lives, while much around them changes. As Dave puts it, from the vantage point of an early retired steelworker:

> When I was part of that 14,000 work force, I was part of a very large family. There were always a lot of things going on. Being on my own now, you don't get the big family feeling that you had when you were part of the steel company.... But there is life after Stelco. And really that's the truth. It's unbelievable, but a number of people plan their whole life around the steel company, and when it's ended found out that, hey, there is other things to do. And they are just as interesting, and there is life, there is life after Stelco. The steel company is never going to be the dominant force in life that it was. Like it's not coming back. (Dave, 1994)

"Contradictory" Consciousness

While rejecting the postmodernist notion of decentered subjectivity, we refuse to fall back upon the modernist version of "Rational man." In private thought and free-flowing discussion, people typically take positions that analysts may describe as being inconsistent. To construct predictable models of rational behaviour, scholars often minimize these contradictions. When people respond in ways we find difficult to explain, when they hold a set of views that confound *our* view of ideological consistency, it is tempting to say that they are confused or even irrational. This is the arrogance of academics more enamoured of abstract model-building, of imposing their own form of reasoning, than listening carefully to the views of ordinary people. Insofar as their experiences are mixed, insofar as they have many commitments and interests which conflict with one another, we have found that our respondents' views reflect this heterogeneity. They gave very diverse answers to a set of questions dealing with what we assumed were closely-related issues of women's and labour's rights. In the statistical analysis (see Livingstone and Mangan, 1996), we did not find, for example, a key question on class or gender issues where knowing people's answer would enable us to predict with significantly increased accuracy how they would respond to other class- or gender-related questions. While a majority indicate a degree of class consciousness involving a basic assertion of labour's rights, this basic disposition does not translate into a unified approach to contract bargaining, co-operation with Stelco management, or the pursuit of shop floor grievances, to say nothing of the class interests of other workers.

Consider one issue: the right to strike. Marxists posit that class conscious workers will express support for the rights of all workers. Among unionized manual workers the general right to strike is often strongly supported. In our 1984 survey, roughly 90% of Stelco workers and their spouses expressed clear support for workers' right to strike without companies hiring replacement workers, an issue of great relevance in the wake of the long 1981 steel strike. The majority also supported the right to strike for teachers, typically on the grounds that they had a similar wage-earning condition. But enthusiasm for the strike principle was subsequently muted by experience and parental interest, even among those, such as our two couples, who expressed the strongest oppositional working-class consciousness,

> The Stelco strike in '81 was the result of two fools. One was the works manager, the other was the union president. Two

> people who would not negotiate with each other in good faith, just through hatred. And we were on strike for four months which crippled the employees and nearly bankrupt the company. We went back for exactly what we turned down early on. You can always have hindsight after a strike, but the common feeling when we went out on this one was that it would be fifteen days, because we were so close.... Acute pig-headedness on both parts, hatred actually. And using 11,000 people as pawns. (Dave, 1984)

Ten years later, the bitter memories of the 1981 strike still lingered more prominently than those of a shorter one in 1990, especially for the women who were pressed into the double workday:

> There should never be a strike like the Stelco 1981 strike. We went three months with no negotiation. There's eleven thousand families, there's a city involved, and it's just a trickle-down effect. There should never, ever be that long, ever. You get what you want in the end sometimes, but nothing is that important to be out of work that long, because the recriminations are worse than the new contract you get. (Donna, 1994)

> It was really hard. We had relatives living with us during the 1981 strike. We tried not to get on each other's case through stress. We held out. The first strike we held down several jobs between us.... We had about five divorces that year.... We can laugh about it now. (Gilda, 1994)

The positive support both couples had expressed for teachers' right to strike in 1984 had been reversed ten years later, after they and their own children had directly experienced their negative effects:

> I disagree with teacher strikes just for the simple fact that it really ruins the kids education, breaks it up. If they re out for a long time, the kid's lost a year. They're delaying the kids education to move on to the world. There should be more and stronger parent-teacher committees to deal with it, be able to voice their opinion over top of the teachers, then I think the teachers would deal with whoever they deal with.... But I

> think teachers need unions, they need protection. In this day and age, the violence in the schools is just phenomenal, which I know about through my community activities. (Greg, 1994)

> No, no. We've been through two teacher strikes. No, definitely not. It really hurt my kids education. My son was in his last year and it finished off the whole year. Then he got caught in another one at college. Absolutely not. (Donna, 1994)

Such shifting attitudes among working-class people over time are likely to be the consequence of direct experiences. When faced with a conflict between two loyalties, they favour the allegiance that is closer to home and more current; in this case, they placed their children's need to get an education, as seen in the short-term, above the teachers' collective bargaining rights which might have benefited their kids in the longer term. An explanation along these lines is consistent with a materialist perspective and much more satisfactory than condemning the confusion, inconsistency and backwardness of the working-class mind.

Through mental classification and the organization of memory, we reduce the scope of the unknown, render life predictable, and facilitate sense-making. The full plenitude of daily life would be intolerable, and taking action impossible, without these simplifying compressions. Since people "make up their minds"- develop classification schemes, sort out disparate impressions, reconcile mixed messages, handle ambiguity and draw conclusions - in a multitude of complex ways, we must grant that rationality, intelligibility, and logical coherence are necessarily multiple. A single standard of rationality is a misleading abstraction. A unilateral notion of true interest is equally idealist. We ought to recognize that the process of producing mental coherence out of the disparate strands of life-experience is the work of individuals, not isolated beings certainly, but thinking actors who place their personal imprint upon the reflective process.

In a modest way, everyone develops their own distinctive view of the world. In the first place, their experiences are to some degree uniquely theirs; furthermore, they register the meaning, they recall and combine the elements of their experience, in different ways. This is not simply the philosophical supposition of naive realists; it is an observable claim about the ongoing mental processes of human beings.

Postmodernism and Postmodernity

The rise of the modern media, beginning with television in the 1950's, is widely heralded as inaugurating the postmodern era. Since we have taken strong exception throughout the text to postmodernism, it is important to make an elementary distinction between *postmodernism* and *postmodernity* (Eagleton, 1996). The latter refers to a new cultural era inaugurated in the last half of the Twentieth Century, marked by "the Information Revolution" and a set of aesthetic shifts in the arts, architecture, fashion, design and entertainment that displaced modernism as the dominant cultural coda of our age, while by no means vanquishing it from the scene entirely. One can dispute the precise nature and scope of this development, celebrate or deplore its various aspects, but the evidence for its rise to prominence is overwhelming. Similarly, there are diverse estimates as to the impact of these transformations upon mass consciousness, but it seems to us indubitable that they are far-reaching, complex and contradictory - full of authoritarian and democratic potential.

Postmodern*ism*, by way of distinction, refers to a general (if heterogenous) style of thought whose ascent can be understood as a response to the cultural mutations outlined above. Developed first in linguistics, literary criticism, studies of popular culture and the media, postmodernism's analytical methods are focused on the "deconstruction" of semiotic phenomena that are treated in most cases as free-floating discourses abstracted from the specific settings of their creation, dissemination and reception. Considered by its proponents to be essential in deciphering the contemporary world, postmodernism has spread throughout the social-science disciplines, being embraced enthusiastically by many academics especially from the disillusioned Left, while drawing vehement rebuttal both from the Right and elements of the Left (Rosenua, 1992; Eagleton, 1996).

Postmodernists have developed many insights, especially in analyses of media-driven discourses. Furthermore, there are currents within the ambit of postmodernism that are drawing back from linguistic idealism and becoming more open to the insights of radical political economy. We have no interest in closing any doors nor exaggerating our differences. But most versions of postmodernist thought appear to us to be idealist, shallow and politically impotent.[58] Too many of its theorists seem to revel in the dazzling surfaces of the commodified universe they seek to deconstruct; this is based on the assumption that, in the postmodern era, appearance rules as never before (Braudillard, 1981). Social reality is submerged beneath "virtual reality" and becomes almost inaccessible. The textual gives way before the visual and the refraction of surface-light occludes depth-perception (Jameson, 1981). Coherence is broken by bewildering fragmentation and holistic social theories lose their persuasiveness. Knowledge gleaned through direct observation and interpersonal communication is overwhelmed by a torrent of transmitted information (and misinformation) from private corporations and states. Everyday consciousness is presumed to have been so thoroughly permeated by technologically enhanced image-making that people's immediate life-circumstances have ceased to be causally basic in forming their identities, shaping their outlooks and loyalties.

From a stance of ironic detachment, most postmodernists imply that there is not very much that we can do about all of this except to remain thoroughly sceptical. The time-honoured cornerstone of progressive social criticism is the revelation of systematic discrepancies between prevailing ideologies and underlying realities to discredit the former and illuminate the latter. This becomes impossible if underlying material realities cannot be adequately discerned much less unveiled, if critical observation cannot be credibly articulated within encompassing frameworks of social explanation. In a world where the interpretive power of established media-driven discourses is not simply dominant but completely overwhelming, the Left's cherished "battle for ideas" is destined to be a side-show, bristling with sound-and-fury but influencing no-one beyond its own dwindling ranks. If "truth is an effect *of* power" (in Foucault's phrase) then it seems wilfully naive to believe that the oppressed could ever find convincing ways to "speak truth *to* power" by uncovering realities obscured by prevailing discourses. How could any social movement or coalition offer a substantial challenge to the image-making dominance of global corporations? And why bother? What is the point of reviving old illusions or replacing them with new ones? Instead, postmodernists remain detached, decoding the semiotic bitstreams that drive public discourse. Such debunking is a valid and important critical function; it may help us to avoid being completely encapsulated by a universe of beguiling images. What multinational corporations and states call "public relations" is now popularly known as "spin-doctoring"; that is a welcome shift in perception. But this progressive role is limited by the refusal to mount a broader critique of the world's new global foundations, since to do so would be to reinstate metanarratives which postmodernists have worked so hard to discredit. This shrivelled ambition reflects an extreme epistemological relativism. Old-fashioned social-scientific work - the careful marshalling of empirical evidence and the rigorous clarification of key concepts - is too often forsaken in the name of polysemy, word games and "undecideability." [59]

Most postmodernists seem far too preoccupied with deconstructing the semiotic plethora of the Information Age to pose deeper questions. Whose interests do the modern media serve? Could they ever be reformed, under insurgent circumstances, to serve the disenfranchised and downtrodden? These old-fashioned concerns are deemed to be too "totalizing" - they cannot be answered except by reproducing a grand narrative, an appealing story about the world that is bound to conceal more than it reveals. While denouncing marxism as a metanarrative with ineradicable totalitarian tendencies, the postmodernists have left largely unexamined the greatest meta-narrative of our time - the neoliberal mantra of the self-regulating free market. Discordant underlying realities, however, still puncture prevailing discourses, just as they always have. In the East Asian financial crisis of 1997, for example, it was capitalism's manifest instabilities, not the critiques of leftist critics, that refuted neoliberalism's creed of market equilibrium and momentarily discredited the *laissez-faire* policy nostrums of the IMF and the World Bank. Future bouts of global economic chaos and "contagion" will do more to revive the flagging fortunes of marxist political economy than all the brilliant treatises leftist intellectuals could ever write.

Mass Media Impacts

With TV sets present in almost every home and most people spending several hours a day watching the tube, there can be no doubt that audiovisual images and messages exert a profound influence on mass consciousness. The subsequent development of personal computers, increasingly linked to one another via the internet, transcends the one-way limits of television and radio; end-users, at least, can speak as well as listen, broadcast as well as receive information. There are positive and negative aspects to all of this. In *The Origins of Postmodernity* (Verso, 1998), Perry Anderson stresses the negative side,

> postmodern culture is not just a set of aesthetic forms it is also a technological package (p. 122). The electronic unification of the earth, instituting the simultaneity of events across the globe as daily spectacle, has lodged a vicarious geography in the recesses of every consciousness, while the encircling networks of multinational capital that actually direct the system exceed the capacities of any perception. (p.56). [The new computer-driven image machinery] are sources of reproduction rather than production... image-resistant themselves, the machines pour out a torrent of images with whose volume no art can compete. The decisive technical environment of the postmodern is constituted by this Niagara of visual gabble. ... But the latter is not simply a wave of images, but also - and above all - of messages... the new apparatuses are perpetual emotion machines transmitting discourses that are wall-to-wall ideology in the strong sense of the term... for the postmodern is ... an index of critical change in the relationship between advanced technology and the popular imaginary (p. 89).

Television viewers are not uncritical consumers of media presentation (Morley, 1996). While viewers do not determine what the networks put on the air, they do select what they wish to watch from available programs. Research has shown that they also engage with programs, interpreting content in their own way (Hobson, 1996). They take special note or conveniently discount, remember or forget, generalize or qualify, according to their own beliefs. They transfer information from one context to another, discussing with others what they have seen and heard in ways that refashion the original message.[60]

Surveys indicate that people are intensely critical of television, believe news reporting to be biassed and hold journalists in low esteem. Noam Chomsky's radical critique of the American media as handmaidens of American foreign policy, for example, is widely accepted far beyond the intellectual Left (1988). It is the form of media presentation, rather than the cognitive content of messages *per se*, that is difficult to treat critically. Most entertainment programs do not persuade by fact and argument but work on a more visceral level, appealing to our fantasies and desires. Advertisements, sitcoms and sports spectacles all work on this level. Their influence upon our consciousness (and the subconscious) is subtle and often hard to discern. We don't change our minds, we just feel differently; our sensibilities have been imperceptibly altered.

Despite their awareness of media bias, viewers get the impression television news coverage operates somewhat differently, that they really do know "what's going on over there. This expands the boundaries of collective identification with, and stereotyping of, remote cultures. In reflecting on television's capacity to extend the horizons of vicarious empathy, Michael Ignatieff (1998, pp. 10-11) appreciates both sides of the equation.

> [With horrifying news coverage of war-ravaged zones and famines in far-away places] television has become the privileged medium through which moral relations between strangers are mediated in the modern world.... On the one hand, television has contributed to the breakdown of the barriers of citizenship, religion, race, and geography that once

> divided our moral space into those we were responsible for and those who were beyond our ken. On the other hand, it makes us voyeurs of the suffering of others, tourists amid their landscapes of anguish. It brings us face-to-face with their fate, while obscuring the distances - social, economic, moral - that lie between us.

But on television's nightly news, this extension of concern to those who are suffering in distant lands is as shallow as it is wide.

> The pell-mell competition to fill the nightly news results in a blur of tragedies and crimes - one minute Afghanistan, the next minute Bosnia, then Rwanda, or a bloody train wreck in Kansas - the cumulative effect is to create a single banalized commodity of horror. The time disciplines of the news genre militate against the minimum moral requirement of engagement with another person's suffering: that one spends time with them, enough time to pierce the carapace of self-absorption and estrangement that separates us from the moral world of others. (Ignatieff, 1998, p. 28)

Left-wing cultural analysts have been intensely critical of television, and justifiably so (Marris and Thornham, 1996). However, the democratic impact of television on politics has often been underestimated. Television images brought the horrors of the Vietnam War into American homes, informed the public's growing opposition to their government's overseas aggression, and hastened the withdrawal of troops in the early 1970's that led ultimately to Washington's defeat. In many countries, the presence of independent television cameras has made dictators more reluctant to massacre their own citizens when thousands take to the streets in unarmed protest; without that threat, the regime's days are often numbered. Ferdinand Marcos was ousted and forced to flee the Phillipines as television, with satellite hook-ups, broadcast mass protests in the streets of Manila whilst his soldiers stood by and watched. The Communist dictatorships of Eastern Europe were peacefully deposed, thanks to the *glasnost* reforms of the Gorbachev regime and the loss of state control over television that made mass protests the subject of sympathetic coverage within these states for the first time. The Chinese government hesitated for ten days as students led mass demonstrations for democracy in Beijing before brutally suppressing them. Who can forget the unscripted TV drama of the solitary protestor walking brazenly in front of a tank, and - equally astonishing - the tank's driver, halting abruptly, saving his life? The collective memory of those days, preserved in television news clips, will one day be revived, inspiring the next round of struggle for democracy in China.

The public discourse on societal problems, produced for and disseminated through the mass media, generally reflects an acceptable spectrum of views concerning the established order, reinforcing prevailing ideologies. In developed capitalist countries with liberal-democratic states, this is not accomplished in a didactic, single-message sense by telling people what to think. Differing views are presented in the mainstream, offering grounds for a limited form of public debate. Taken together, they offer no fundamental challenge to the prevailing order. Moderate views are promoted, rendered respectable and worthy of serious consideration, while radical voices are marginalised, their spokespersons discounted as being "beyond the pale."

The commercial media channel public attention away from an exploration of the root causes of popular discontent and strategic alternatives to focus narrowly on tactical choices; instead of a wide-ranging discussion of policy issues, they become fixated on prominent personalities and on handicapping electoral races; rather than examining the ways and means of promoting systemic change, they call for the replacement of discredited leaders with others of slightly different persuasion (Leys, 1999). Only in the specialized field of academic publishing, with limited audiences, is a wider array of views respectfully heard, their authors treated as legitimate participants.

The interests of subordinate groups are often subsumed in mainstream accounts.[61] In liberal discourses, they tend to be included by universal abstraction in which the representatives of dominant groups speak for us all. Hence, women become part of mankind; workers part of the company; minorities are Canadian citizens, regardless of race. From the moderate Left, they are treated sympathetically; from the Right, they are frequently blamed for society's ills. Rarely, across this limited spectrum, are they empowered to speak in their own voices and granted more than twenty seconds to explain their views.

While people are inhibited from drawing radical conclusions by the construction of mainstream discourse, these limits are not comprehensive. The entire edifice, while powerful, is also porous and riven by contradictions that provide avenues to marginalised and more radical viewpoints. Widespread dissent and popular ferment can broaden the grounds of mainstream public discourse from below, just as elite pressure may narrow the framework from above. Working-class skepticism about the mass media are strongly suggested by some of the comments of our couples. For example:

> So the newspapers have all come out against it, so what? I don't know, I don t even bother myself with it. I don t even read newspapers. I just ignore it. (Greg, 1984)

> My political views are starting to change. Like I was strictly NDP. But, as government, I think they've really screwed the work force when they were supposed to be the one to back the work force. Now I get at it with all sorts of politicians and I'm up in the air right now. It's a big decision for me because I never used to care about politics because my dad was always NDP. But now when an election comes around I am forever reading up on what is happening. I never used to do that. (Greg, 1994)

> I don't think things are as bad in Canada as the two minute news blurb you hear at night, what went on. I just think we have far more access to it now. It's mostly political trivia. Look at history - governments have always been run by slightly eccentric people. I think the biggest problem is envi-

ronmental, more and more environmental accidents that sooner or later are going to cost hundreds of thousands of lives. And then we're going to wake up. And that's my greatest concern, for the future. (Dave, 1984)

Market Atomization and Assertions of Collective Identity

The experience of being surrounded on all sides by markets - of having to secure one's livelihood and obtain most of life's necessary goods and services through market exchange - fosters a strong sense that everyone's top priority must be "to look out for Number One," however generous and group-minded individuals are otherwise inclined to be. Possessive individualism, and the form of calculative rationality it sponsors, resists subordinating one's interests or identity for the sake of the collective project (Macpherson, 1962).

One of the principal individualist incentives that has undermined labour solidarity has been the opportunity to work overtime afforded by companies such as Stelco. During the 1980's and early 90's, even in the midst of mass layoffs, overtime work increased for the employed work force.[62] Class conscious workers like Dave and Greg have wrestled deeply with this problem, both in terms of an effective collective response and an individual choice.

The company's view is for every person they bring back off the street, it costs $5,000. So, pay overtime, it's cheaper. There's now an underground workers' movement who are compiling lists of laid off steel workers with lists of people who are filling their jobs on overtime. It's being mailed out to them.... It's probably a futile thing but I'm a hundred percent in agreement with it. It's, I don't know, it's very, very frustrating when you see people working overtime and taking home added paychecks. And you know several people who were on your crew for many years are laid off. They've got a house and kids and it s very disturbing. But when they say there's overtime, they get a line-up a mile long. It's frustrating, very frustrating. (Dave, 1984)

> As far as I'm concerned, guys that work overtime should be fined through the union. I disagree with it altogether. Like, I had opportunities to work overtime but I wouldn't because there are guys out on the street. I m working but they re not and they re in the same boat as I am. There are senior guys who should be retired, working overtime like crazy. I don't buy that. I have seen fights start over it, too. We had a guy work twenty-four hours straight the other day. Sick.(Greg, 1984)

> Overtime is still running rampant in our department. It's crazy. But now I ve finally started working it, after they called everybody back. Other than that, I was dead set against it. Being younger with a lower wage, people looked at me and said "what, are you, nuts?" I just totally disagree because of, you know, the union. Guys were laid off, why should I be doing their jobs? It's just totally, it's outrageous actually. I know guys who are doing seventy hours in one pay. The union can't control it. Now the general attitude is if I don't do it, then somebody else is going to do it, anyway. So why not grab it while I can.... I used to pound everybody all the time for working it. Now since I started working it, I got scab written all over my locker, but it's all in fun. Sometimes it got pretty heated with certain guys. But then it was forgotten about the next day. Like you got to work with these guys and no sense being mad at each other. (Greg, 1994)[63]

The choices people make in these self-defining moments cannot be determined by reference to their "true" interests as if a singular course of action was suggested by the situation that all rational actors would naturally pursue in the circumstances. All responses involve intrinsic value judgments as well as differing assessments of the situation. Inevitably, people's actions have a moral dimension, involving their sense of fairness and loyalty, their vision of a just and democratic society.

The process of competitive atomisation - dissolving traditional communities and inducing people to rely upon a narrow calculus of self-interest - has been rolling over the globe for centuries, seeping into every corner of social life.[64] Throughout the modern era, our deepening immersion in market relations has been feared and deplored by analysts across the political spectrum, lamenting the loss of locally-based communities in the midst of a mass urban culture of anonymity and commodity abstraction. The sense of uprootedness and personal disorientation in the face of breakneck change and cultural fragmentation is central to the experience of modernity, where "all that is solid melts into air" (Marx, 1974a, p. 70).

In the past two decades, the process has accelerated.[65] As economic growth has slowed since the mid 1970's, the pressure on people to compete has been growing. Employment insecurity has been intensified by cuts in government social programs. People's financial worries about job security and personal debt combine with other apprehensions, such as the future of our children's schools and women's safety walking home at night.

These anxieties are exacerbated by an intense frustration, in many cases a thorough-going cynicism, with politics. Who can we hold accountable? Who can we count on to put things right? There is a widespread perception across the ideological spectrum that political parties, once in office, will break their promises. Regardless of the platform they ran on, they will all end up doing basically the same thing once they are elected. Our electoral choices seem nearly meaningless.[66] The best-laid plans of finance departments and central banks are regularly capsized by currency speculators, cross-border capital surges, and debt repayment jitters which can rapidly degenerate into liquidity crises (as in Mexico in January 1995). Less and less do governments set their nations' agenda; they react to the movements of international capital, scurrying to adopt the increasingly harsh remedies prescribed for the ills of the public sector by the new kingpins of the private sector, the global money managers and bond-rating agencies (Seccombe, 1999).

Large sections of the population are suffering and feeling vulnerable, their life-chances held hostage to a process of ruthless international competition and global restructuring. They don t need left-wing analysts to tell them that there is no invisible hand benevolently guiding the tiller of the world economy. With every new plant shutdown, company bankruptcy, currency collapse and ecological disaster, they can see that the economy runs out of control, beyond the effective capacity of working people, communities, and even national governments to shape for the collective benefit of citizens. Even though, since 1992, economic growth has resumed and official unemployment has declined, there remains a pervasive sense of foreboding concerning the future. Polls indicate that large numbers of people expect to be financially worse off in a decade than they are now. Intensified competition and resulting insecurity exacerbates fears, resentment and scapegoating blaming those who threaten one's position from below, such as women and minorities favoured by affirmative action schemes.

These disintegrative processes of atomisation and recrimination encounter various forms of resistance. Even for those of us who are not depressed materially, the marketplace fails to meet basic social needs for long-term relationships based on co-operation, trust and respect. Feeling increasingly vulnerable, we are not inclined to "go it alone" but to reach out for others. In periods when people turn away from public remedies and collective action, they seek refuge in the intimacy of family and close friends. Most of us deeply value, and strive hard to preserve, reliable life-long bonds of family and friendship. Ideally, these relationships are based upon principles of loyalty and generalized obligation rather than the limited liability, "get-it-in-writing" contracts that are marketplace standards. While the principles of market exchange - where the watchword is: "what have you done for me lately?" - are increasingly evident in social relationships, people continue to resist the dissolution of long-standing commitments and a sense of community. For Greg, community work has become something of a personal crusade:

> When I come home from work, that's when the fun starts. I'm into everything. I'm heavily involved with several community organizations, hours every day.... Once I got involved in what I could do about the community and I started working with other people on it, it just evolved and now it's a full-blown program for me. I have a lot of fun, I met a lot of people. I deal with a lot of kids and stuff like that. It's very interesting. Greg, 1994)

Dave and Donna are much less active, but they feel a similar social need:

> They need more recreation centres, especially for the young people to get them off the streets. They need to do something to make people proud to be Hamiltonian, because they're not. (Donna, 1994)

> When it all becomes broken down into small individual things going on, then there's got to be some way of getting it back as a community. (Dave, 1994)

While modern capitalism tends to disintegrate traditional, locally-based communities, the system's driving forces also generate pressures which foster group awareness and offer opportunities to take collective action which extend beyond local, face-to-face relations. Recent technological revolutions - in travel, trade and communications - have shortened distance and facilitated the formation of wide-ranging associations in ways that were impractical, indeed inconceivable, not long ago. The global sway of transnational corporations, the rapid growth of world trade, the strengthening of international trade agreements and trading blocs, the sweeping integration of the world's financial markets - all of this has generated enormous centralizing pressures across the nations of the industrialised world.

While fomenting conflict, division and competitive rivalry, these trends have nonetheless forced a harmonization of government policy, increasing conformity in state regulation, convergence of socio-economic conditions and the homogenization of media-driven cultural forms. In turn, these convergences have stimulated the formation of all sorts of loosely organized coalitions to seek things that the free market fails to offer or places at risk, such as more equality, a reduced work-week, national self-determination, or clean water. It is gradually becoming easier to tie local community resistance into nation-wide networks and international coalitions promoting children's rights, opposition to genetically modified foods, the cancellation of the government debt in poor countries, and so on.[67]

Forms of Social Struggle

In his analysis of the small-holding peasants of France in *The Eighteenth Brumaire of Louis Bonaparte*, Marx states, in consecutive sentences, that they form a class but do not form a class. He seems to be suggesting his famous distinction between a class-in-itself and class-for-itself:

> In so far as millions of families live under economic conditions of existence that separate their mode of life, their interests and their cultural formation from those of other classes and bring them into conflict with those classes, they form a class. In so far as these small peasant-proprietors are merely connected on a local basis, and the identity of their interests fails to produce a feeling of community, national links, or a political organization, they do not form a class. They are therefore incapable of asserting their class interest in their own name, whether through a parliament or through a convention. They cannot represent themselves, they must be represented. (1974b, p. 239).

The key ingredients mentioned here in transforming an atomized and politically inert subordinate class into an effective force capable of asserting its interests on a nation-wide basis are: the cultural formation of community; networks of affiliation extending between communities to forge national links; and political organization.

We need to recognize the indispensable role of national organizations in bringing disparate communities and sectors together in common cause. Even as global capitalism limits national sovereignty, nation-states proliferate; popular movements cannot circumvent the state. There is simply no viable alternative to exerting pressure upon governments, and ultimately contesting state power, at the national level. Typically, national parties and other types of political organization require tremendous collective effort to get started and to be built, branch by branch, across a country.

Political parties and movement organizations are often much more enduring than the forces that animate them. Once they have established permanent infrastructures and are in a position to deliver minimal services to active members on an ongoing basis, they do not require nearly as much energy from the grass roots to sustain. This is how they endure through quiescent periods when active support wanes. When a new wave of struggle arises, established organizations strive to adapt so as to gain the support of a new generation of activists. Given the difficulties of building new national structures from scratch, the mere presence of veteran political organizations provides an opportunity for renewal, as younger activists enter in droves, take over local branches, and eventually make their presence felt at the national level. The constancy of parties and movement organizations should not be confused with a homogeneity of membership and steadfastness of purpose over time; more often, it is a case of new wine refilling old bottles.

The development of a revolutionary alternative requires the formation of a social movement and a protracted period of collective struggle. One problem with sustaining radical perspectives among a large mass of people, however, is that they find it depressing to focus relentlessly on the causes and conditions of their oppression. A radical viewpoint may be especially unappealing when it seems impossible to put an end to one's suffering in the near future. People are normally inclined to adopt more moderate and optimistic outlooks, enabling them to remain hopeful that their situation may be substantially improved without engaging in a major fight with attendant risks and sacrifices. In order to get on with their lives, subordinates normally prefer to stay out of trouble. Their compliance is much more likely to be secured through the "dull compulsions of everyday life," and a pragmatic aversion to taking imprudent risks, than by an abiding faith in existing institutions and leaders (Mann, 1970, pp. 423-39; Abercrombie, Hill & Turner, 1980).

In any conception of collective struggle, it is important to distinguish between persistent forms of resistance which may bend but do not break the routines of daily life, and open fights, episodic in nature, which radically disrupt work-rules and constituted authority. Various forms of resistance - sullen "foot-dragging," clandestine sabotage, "accidents," inattention and sloppiness - are predicated on a threshold of grievance, a determination to contest, and the capacity to "walk a tightrope" between dutiful compliance and open defiance.

During long periods of surface conformity, when daily routines are in place, the grievances of the oppressed accumulate. The "hidden injuries of class" fester. Subordinates resent the arrogance, condescension and hypocrisy of their superiors. They suffer in silence the lack of dignity and respect accorded them. Once an individual or small group stands up and openly fights an injustice, however, the backlog of grievances find fresh voice and long-suppressed indignation surfaces. As soon as it appears that the authorities are divided or vacillating, that a strong show of unity and determination might win the day, the barriers of silence and resignation crack open. The militant minority now find that they have a much more receptive audience for their combative proposals, as their normally moderate associates look to them for leadership in a crisis. The exemplary defiance of the few rapidly becomes the rebellion of the many. The spread of such fury like wildfire, once the momentum begins to build and the balance of forces tilts, may take everyone by surprise, even the participants.[68]

This dynamic view of the explosive potential of mass consciousness has been informed in the twentieth century by psychoanalytic insights, especially an appreciation of the layered and conflicted nature of human consciousness. Wilhelm Reich, in particular, explored the potential, both progressive and reactionary, of the return of the unconscious in the midst of political crises in Germany, when the routines of daily life were disrupted and the rules of conformity, of deference to authority, were temporarily shattered.[69] In these extraordinarily fluid moments, the combative impulses of large numbers of people erupt into consciousness with astonishing rapidity, transforming apparently meek people into angry rebels, radicalizing their formerly conventional outlooks. Working in the shadow of an insurgent fascist movement, Reich was not naively enthused by this prospect, realizing that the widespread return of the unconscious would manifest both regressive and emancipatory tendencies; it could unleash mass energies fuelling a political radicalization to the right or to the left. All that was certain was that such eruptions would break the mould of conventional politics and lead to a sharp polarization of perspectives which would disintegrate the "normal" (bell curve) distribution of viewpoints around a "sober centre" of the ideological spectrum.

This thesis concerning the dynamic consciousness of the oppressed retains its general validity. History provides numerous examples, most recently the mass rebellion against the authority of the clerical elite in Iran. The transport workers' strike in France in late 1995 elicited widespread support from other unionized workers and the general public, bringing much of the country to a standstill for a month. Once again, the spontaneous scope of the struggle was completely unexpected. The classical marxist strategy of overthrowing capitalist power by means of proletarian insurrection was predicated upon this volcanic potential. In light of the difficulty of developing a counter-hegemonic alternative, however, its implications for the prospects of *successful* revolt and the construction of a new social order qualitatively in advance of the old are not nearly as optimistic as marxists have traditionally supposed.

The two working-class couples whose experience and expressions of group consciousness directly inform our analysis suggest that most of their work-mates do not care about union politics most of the time. But they harbour a deep sense of grievance against their companies exploitative treatment of them as human beings. As we have seen, this is far from their only sentiment about capitalists or capitalism. Their common posture to open struggle against their employer is best expressed by Dave, the veteran trade union activist:

> There may not be a strong spirit of unionism in the membership, not right now. Right now, everyone's out to cover his own ass, basically. And it's only natural. What do I have to do to survive, myself? And right now that s the way it is, and you see it over and over again.... But the spirit is always there, anytime there s a *cause*. You require some sort of a cause for the people to wrap themselves together. (Dave, 1984)

In the present period, there are clearly great difficulties involved in building coalitions from below where subordinate groups find ways to "wrap themselves together" to make common cause.[70] For the core of the working-class, rising income inequality heightens awareness of, and thereby increases the fear of falling into, the underclass. Work-mates dispersed by layoffs can soon be forgotten. While white working-class people are more supportive of racial equality than conventional stereotypes suggest, alliances with visible minorities remain seriously blocked by lack of familiarity, limited awareness of systemic features of race discrimination, and a fear of unfair competition for scarce jobs. Similarly, working-class men and women, like most others, exhibit strong generational differences in their extent of support for gender equity and affirmative action policies in hiring and promotion. The divisions that narrow the vision of working people and limit their enthusiasm for collective action arise from their material conditions as do their oppositional consciousness and periodic willingness to reach out and extend a hand of solidarity to those beneath them in the social order.

Conclusion: The Possibility of Transformative Class Consciousness

In *What Is To Be Done*, Lenin made the distinction between economic (or trade union) consciousness and class political consciousness. The former was generated by the collective struggle of the workers against their employers for better terms in the sale of their labour power (p. 167); the latter originated outside the sphere of relations between workers and employers... in the sphere of relationships of *all* classes and strata to the state and the government (p. 182). In a polemic against the Economists who wanted to concentrate the party's efforts on trade union struggles, Lenin (1970) sought to expose workers:

> to every manifestation of tyranny and oppression, no matter where it appears, no matter what stratum or class of people it affects; ... to generalize all these manifestations and produce a single picture of police violence and capitalist exploitation (p. 174).

His goal was to stimulate among workers an empathy for all of the oppressed, so that:

> the most backward worker will understand, *or will feel*, that the students and religious sects, the peasants and the authors are being abused and outraged by those same dark forces that are oppressing and crushing him at every step of his life (p. 175). [In this way, the marxist party would be able] to gather and concentrate all these drops and streamlets of popular

> resentment that are brought forth to a far greater extent than we imagine by the conditions of Russian life ... and [combine them] into a *single* gigantic torrent (p. 181).

As it turned out, Lenin's conception of class political knowledge, disseminated *by the party* from outside the workers' sphere, played a fateful role in the authoritarian development of Stalinism in the Soviet Union and around the world. Yet the original distinction between a narrow, self- limiting form of oppositional consciousness and a far-reaching transformative (or counter-hegemonic) consciousness, which is well-informed about, and empathetic with, the striving of oppressed groups, remains a compelling one today.

As our research has demonstrated, there are presently few signs of a transformative class consciousness among the Hamilton working-class. Fundamental to any effective counter-hegemonic strategy, in our view, is for the core of the labour movement to reach out and build enduring alliances with the poor and the unemployed, as well as with the feminist and civil rights movements. Temporary alliances have occurred in the past and some progressive labour organizations have been trying heroically for many years to build social unionism alone these lines.[67] Significant progress requires that social activists recognize the real contours of contemporary consciousness of class, gender and racial differences. Bridges of solidarity will need to be built across deep gulfs, especially between the white, male-dominated core of the industrial unions and the non-white, largely female workers in the lower strata of the unorganized working-class.

The changes associated with global restructuring can cut both ways. As Charles Spencer (1978:242), a veteran steel mill-hand, reminds us:

> It is often easy to misjudge the early signs of social change. It is easy to be silent about the blue collar workers, who are far down at the bottom of the social heap. And, for those whose profession it is to govern the state, the temptations have always been to be concerned only with its top surface layers, the rich, the educated, the powerful. But sooner or later the world will shift.

The yearning for alternatives to the established order have not been extinguished in the working-class. There is popular support for co-operative forms of business ownership, more effective use of workers' knowledge and creative initiative in the workplace, a shorter work-week to redistribute available work and lower unemployment, and a fairer division of labour between spouses on the home front (see Livingstone, 1999; Freeman and Rogers, 1999). The level of support for such progressive changes is typically highest among the rapidly growing numbers of underemployed workers (Livingstone, 1999, p. 273):

> We need a society which puts humans first, not money.... There needs to be more coordinated planning among governments, schools and colleges, and business. But businesses are not taking the initiative at all.... The people who control things need a massive dose of education to bring them down to the human level as opposed to a preoccupation with money. (Underemployed middle-aged service worker with a university degree)

There are also encouraging signs in the growing participation of rank-and-file workers in their unions' courses and opportunities for informal learning. A worker who has recently taken the Canadian Auto Workers' paid education leave program (PEL) comments:

> The way PEL really contributes would be [reflected in] the idea of humanity I try to show the people I work with. Since Scarborough [Ontario's GM van plant] closed, we have a lot of minority cultures.... I try to show them some kind of a welcome. That's another point from PEL too; I'm tending to 'all trade unionists are the same.' So I ended up spending some time on other workers' picket-lines, I talked with those people, and I dropped into a plant demonstration because it was a labour strife issue and I felt... I wanted to be there. I sort of have sympathy... I just sort of feel for these guys. They've been jerked around by a corporation that's making lots of money and there's no reason for it. I can't see the underdog go like that (Livingstone and Roth, 1998, p.20).

This worker's sentiments extend well beyond the traditional form of trade union activism on "bread and butter" issues to embrace the need for a much broader solidarity with oppressed groups as their common problems become more pressing.

In creative response to the underlying dynamics of the global economy and system of nation-states, subordinated people continue to recast their personal aspirations and larger social dreams. Whether, when and how their deep "down-to-earth" resentments of the system's inequities will provoke them to reach out to link up with either progressive or regressive movements for social change remain central political questions of our time.

Appendix: The Hamilton Interviews

In 1983, our project drew a representative sample of about 200 steelworkers and their wives or partners was drawn, using USWA Local 1005's membership lists of 13,000 hourly-rated workers at Stelco's Hilton Works. We gave respondents give an extensive questionnaire covering their paid work, domestic labour and community experiences as well as a wide array of social attitudes, and we followed this up in 1984 with in-depth interviews of a subsample of over forty respondents, covering their coping strategies during the period of layoffs and restructuring.

In 1984 we also conducted separate interviews with over twenty of the women who were among the female steelworkers hired at Stelco in 1980, as a result of the "Women Back into Stelco" Campaign. Finally, we carried out a survey of the entire Hamilton population of co-resident adult couples. The respondents to this survey, based on a stratified random sample (N=798), answered a questionnaire that contained many of the same questions as the prior steelworker questionnaire. One unusual feature of these questionnaires was that they went into much greater depth than most such surveys about both the actual working conditions and workplace authority relations of respondents, as well as various facets of their social and political attitudes. On the basis of these questions, class locations and consciousness scores were assigned as described in Sections II and III here.

The survey responses were weighted to compensate for slight discrepancies in response rates across the census tracts; all figures for the 1984 data are from the weighted samples, and small rounding errors may appear. The basic findings of this survey are presented in Corman, Livingstone, Luxton, & Seccombe, (1985).

In 1989 Elizabeth Asner conducted follow-up telephone interviews of a sub-sample of intermediate-class women selected from the hamilton-wide survey. Asner 1993 analyses thee interviews in detail. In 1994, Belinda Leach, Niamh Hennessey, and D.W. Livingstone conducted follow-up in-depth interviews with a range of the people interviewed a decade earlier, including over 20 couples. These interviews form the basis for much of the evidence presented in this volume.

Notes

1. Ernesto Laclau and Chantal Mouffe (1985) have deeply influenced, and come to exemplify, the movement of radical intellectuals away from marxism towards identity politics. See especially, *Hegemony and Socialist Strategy, Towards a Radical Democratic Politics*, London, Verso, 1985. Norman Geras offers a marxist rebuttal in 'Ex-Marxism Without Substance: Being a Real Reply to Laclau and Mouffe,' *New Left Review*, 169, 1988, pp. 34-61.
2. On the kaleidoscopic phenomena of postmodernisty, Fredric Jameson (1991) is an intellectual feast. David Harvey (1990) ties postmodernisty to underlying socio-economic transitions and the acceleration of spatial and temporal compression in developed capitalist formations. John McGowan (1991) surveys the intellectual terrain of postmodernism, drawing out the implications of various positions for an emancipatory politics.
3. The revamped parties of the Right (associated with the Thatcher government in Britain and the Reagan Administration in the United States) are frequently called neo-conservative, especially in North America. This designation flows logically from the conventional map of the political spectrum where conservatism appears on the Right, liberalism occupies the Centre ground and social-democracy is situated on the (mainstream) Left. We prefer to call the new champions of *laissez-faire* capitalism "neo-liberal" because it more accurately describes their ideology. The basic project of these parties has been to reduce the role of the State in the economy, freeing markets from government regulation. These goals were integral to classical liberalism. In the Nineteenth Century, they were often pursued against the strenuous objections of conservative parties who defended an ideal of the integral community against market atomism and the rise of possessive individualism. The modern-day advocates of this stance on the Right are often termed "social conservatives" to distinguish them from economic libertarians.
4. See Manfred Garhammer, *Time and Society*, vol. 4, # 2.
5. From a Statistics Canada study by Mike Sheridan, Deborah Sunter and Brent Diverty, reported in the *Globe & Mail*, September 2,1996.
6. Canadians got poorer in the 90s, *Globe & Mail*, May 13, 1998, p. A 5.
7. The phrase is from Barbara Ehrenreich, *Fear of Falling: The Inner Life of the Middle Class*. New York: Pantheon, 1989.
8. In the 1997 federal election, more union members voted for the Reform Party than the New Democratic Party (cited in the *Globe & Mail*, August 28, 1999, p. A4).
9. This is a rough estimate based upon comments of USWA Local 1005 members on the 1990 strike picket lines and the finding that nearly all the women homemakers in our 1984 interviews were in paid employment when re-interviewed in 1994.
10. This is the core insight we take from postmodernist thought: the way in which power relations are reproduced within a discourse of binary opposition between "us and them," and the latter category, "the other," is rendered alien and debased. It is an especially telling critique of the philosophical foundations of Western thought which abound with either/or couplets of mutual exclusion and false

dichotomy. From Hegel through Marx to Habermas, many radical philosophers have mounted powerful critiques of the cherished dichotomies of Western thought. Undaunted by the risks of conceptual reification which now haunt the postmodernists, they moved beyond negation to propose dialectical reformulations (i.e., the synthesis of opposites). Nowadays, most postmodernists dismiss all such revision as "meta-narratives." Their thrust is thus overwhelmingly negative: to deconstruct, displace and delegitimate, but rarely to propose alternatives. The purpose of this refusal is to respect *"différence"* by blocking conceptual reincorporation by dominant discourses; the effect, too often, is to strand us on our islands of difference, with no way to think about shared aspects of our condition or to prepare the political grounds of coalescent action.

11. Obviously, we are here repudiating a central tenet of orthodox marxism's faith in the centrality of class struggle. This seems to us to have been more a product of "manifesto marxism" (with pithy excerpts from a handful of famous texts used to introduce new recruits to the Communist Party's boundless confidence in the revolutionary proletariat) than of a careful reading of a full range of historical materialism's more reflective and analytical texts. Less obviously, the refusal to forecast inexorable trends also counters the post-marxist farewell to the proletariat (Gorz 1982), which writes off this class's future contribution to human emancipation.

12. 'Bombs a Betrayal for Dissident Serbs,' *Globe & Mail*, May 22, 1999, p. A 17.

13. "The mode of production of material life determines the general character of the social, political, and spiritual processes of life. It is not the consciousness of men that determine their being, but their being that determine their consciousness." Marx, 1963, p. 67.

14. See *The Struggle for Recognition, the Moral Grammar of Social Conflicts*, by Axel Honneth, MIT Press, Cambridge, Mass., 1996.

15. Lenin developed this argument in the midst of the bitter split with the Second International where, on the eve of the First World War, the social-democratic parties had supported the military-imperial ventures of their national governments, betraying the principles of proletarian internationalism.

16. These issues are insightfully reviewed in the introduction to *Challenging Authority, the Historical Study of Contentious Politics*, edited by Michael P. Hanagan, Leslie Page Moch, and Wayne Te Brake, University of Minnesota Press, Minneapolis, 1998.

17. "Intense feelings of grievance alone do not provoke mass discord; only the prospect of success in addressing them leads large numbers to commit the time for and take the risks of mass action." In 'Tactical Information and the Diffusion of Peaceful Protests' by Stuart Hill, Donald Rothchild and Colin Cameron, chapter 3 of *The International Spread of Ethnic Conflict, Fear, Diffusion and Escalation*, David A. Lake & Donald Rothchild, eds., Princeton University Press, 1998, p. 66. The authors cite numerous studies that make the same point.

18. It is unfortunate that interest- and identity-based accounts are so polarized today; our efforts have been inspired by a minority of progressive social theorists such as Nancy Fraser who have been working diligently to bridge the gap (c.f., *Justice Interruptus, Critical Reflections in the "Postsocialist" Condition*, Routledge, 1997). While we do not claim to have achieved a full theoretical

integration in this text, we have sought to lay the groundwork for doing so by presenting a fairly extensive revision of the marxist conception of material interest.
19. See, most fundamentally, Sigmund Freud's *The Ego and The Id*, London, Hogarth Press, 1923. The implications for European culture are explored in *Civilization and Its Discontents*, New York, Cape & Smith, 1930. Jean Piaget's works are widely published; on the development of causal reasoning in children, see *The Construction of Reality in the Child*, New York, Basic Books, 1954.
20. Sigmund Freud, *Beyond the Pleasure Principle*, London, Hogarth Press, [1920], 1955.
21. Marx was not blind to these divisive processes, but he thought that they would be overcome by homogenizing forces, some intrinsic to capitalist development, and others the result of the deliberate efforts of the most class conscious workers to forge a broad unity within the labour movement. "This organization of the proletarians into a class... is constantly being upset again by the competition between workers themselves. But it rises up again, stronger, firmer, mightier." (1974a, p. 76). It was the aspiration of marxists to create the framework within which the dispersed wisdom of the international working-class could be brought together, codified in "lessons of struggle," and widely disseminated.
22. Marx's hostility to "the lumpenproletariat" was often quite extreme: "the 'dangerous class,' the social scum, that passively rotting mass thrown off by the lowest layers of the old society, may, here and there, be swept into the movement by a proletarian revolution; its conditions of life, however, prepare it far more for the part of a bribed tool of reactionary intrigue." (1974a, p. 77.) His views, in this respect, were typical of the propertied classes of his time.
23. For a thorough documentation of these relationships in U.S. inner city ghettos, see Wilson, 1993.
24. For a preliminary version of an expanded conception of socio-economic positions, including class cores and peripheries, see Livingstone. 1983.
25. Armstrong, Glyn and Harrison (1984) present this long-wave sequence for developed capitalist countries, with impressive empirical documentation.
26. See the discussion of the male breadwinner family norm in Seccombe, 1993. pp. 111-24.
27. "The production of ideas, conceptions, and consciousness is at first directly interwoven with material activity and the material intercourse of men, the language of real life... Morality, religion, metaphysics, and other ideologies, and their corresponding forms of consciousness, no longer retain their appearance of autonomous existence.... It is men, who, in developing their material production and their material intercourse, change, along with this their real existence, their thinking and the products of their thinking." Marx, 1963, p. 90.
28. See 'Sources of Variation in Working-Class Movements in Twentieth-Century Europe,' Michael Mann , *New Left Review*, # 212, July/August 1995, p. 14.
29. Several theorists have made the distinction we make between lower levels of consciousness, "the whole aggregate of life experiences and the outward expressions directly connected with it... unsystematised and unfixed inner and outer speech" (in the words of Voloshinov) and upper levels. See, for example, Eagleton, 1991, pp.48-9. Our research drew upon both realms. At the outset of our

initial interview, we asked people to 'walk us through' their daily lives to understand the relationship between the routine demands of daily life and the practical consciousness they exercise in coping with these demands, monitoring the situation, making decisions and co-ordinating their activities with others. Then at the end of the questionnaire and during follow-up interviews, we asked people to locate themselves in the class structure, to state an opinion on the rights and responsibilities of various groups in society, the nature of social conflict in Canada and their vision of a preferred future for the country.

30. In the Sausserian scheme: "what we generally call the signified - the meaning or conceptual content of an utterance - is now seen as a meaning-effect, as that objective mirage of signification generated and projected by the relationship of signifiers among themselves." (Jameson, 1991, p. 26).

31. An additional problem has been the imperial tendency of the postmodernists (while deriding the meta-narratives of others) to cast material forms and practices in the language of discourse. The built-space of cities is "architectural discourse," and so on; almost everything is "discursively constituted" because its meaning is conveyed through language.

32. The problem of ahistorical sociology is compounded by the current infatuation with the "four posts" - post-industrial, post-Fordism, post-structuralism and postmodernity. These terms ostensibly tell us what the current context comes *after* without telling us anything specific about the present period itself; they make the contemporary world seem profoundly discontinuous from all that has gone before.

33. It must be recognized, however, that the presence of statistically significant correlations rarely accounts for a majority of the variance displayed in the sample; secondly, the existence of a non-coincidental association can never prove a direct cause and effect relationship between the variables in question. We can safely *infer* a causal connection between people's social location and consciousness, but we can never definitively show *why* the members of a certain group are more likely than those in other groups or positions to adopt specific views.

34. For detailed accounts of the construction of measures of oppositional class consciousness and fuller analyses of their incidence in Hamilton, see chapter one in Livingstone and Mangan (1996).

35. In respecting the confidentiality of our respondents, we have given them pseudonyms and rendered certain biographical details in the following portraits vague. A limitation of the interviews is that our approach was routed through the steelworkers' union local and our first contact was therefore with the male steelworker in most cases. Partly because of this and partly because of their continuing male breadwinner power, their voices are predominant on topics related to the work place.

36. In his theoretical works (such as *Capital, Volume 1*), Marx employs a bi-polar model of opposing classes - a subordinated class of direct producers and a dominant class appropriating the surplus - applicable, in a general sense, to the analysis of all class-based modes of production. By contrast, in his historical works (such as *The Eighteenth Brumaire of Louis Bonaparte*), when he is analyzing entire social formations in an ongoing political drama, he portrays a much fuller ensemble, complete with class fractions, shifting alignments of interest from one

conjuncture to the next, and political alliances forged between classes reflecting and sealing these shifts. The distance between these levels of analysis is actually very considerable, but it has not been adequately recognized. We have tended to accept uncritically Marx's prediction that the development of Modern Industry (as he put it) would simplify the class structure of mature capitalist formations as intermediate, petit-bourgeois, classes declined. This structural simplification has not occurred; new intermediate strata have emerged and small family businesses have continued to occupy an important economic niche. See the discussion of this more complex class structure within production relations, complete with documentation for Hamilton, in chapter 1 of Livingstone and Mangan (1996).

37. For detailed accounts of management-labour relations at Stelco's Hilton Works, see Corman et al., 1993 and Livingstone, 1996.

38. The source of their outlook was therefore held to be extrinsic to the situation and its appeal a chimera. Significantly, this explanation mirrors the account that conservative ideologues frequently offer of working-class rebellions - that they are not based on genuine grievances, but are triggered by the demagogy of "outside agitators" who whip up mob frenzy and induce normally sensible workers to act irrationally. When some feminists claim that conservative women have been "seduced by patriarchy" or black activists deride African-Canadians whose "minds have been whitewashed," they do not illuminate the consciousness of conservative women or blacks any better than marxists have the views of working-class supporters of the Reform Party.

39. The marxist scholar Eugene Genovese (1972) explored the terrain of intimate interdependence between starkly unequal partners in *Roll Jordan Roll*, his insightful portrait of the relations between slaves and masters in the Ante-Bellum South. We readily acknowledge the influence of his work on our own thinking in this text.

40. Comparing her respondents' views in the 1970s with their outlook in the 1990s, Lillian Rubin has traced a parallel shift in the consciousness of white working-class Americans: rising economic insecurity, staunch defence of their traditional labour market prerogatives, resentment at affirmative action and a loss of empathy with the black underclass. The former study is presented in *Worlds of Pain, Life in the Working-Class Family* (Basic Books, 1976); the latter in *Families on the Faultline, America's Working-class Speaks About the Family, the Economy, Race, and Ethnicity* (Harper Collins, 1994).

41. See the similar recent interpretations of the impact of civil rights legislation among the U.S. white working-class as documented by Rubin (1994).

42. Cited in the Globe & Mail, January 3, 1997, p. A4.

43. As James C. Scott suggests (1990, p. 223): "For most subordinate groups, the social relations in which one can speak with real safety are narrowly restricted. Generally speaking, the smaller and more intimate the group, the safer the possibilities for free expression. The more effective the dominant groups are in preventing subordinates from assembling in substantial numbers free of surveillance, the smaller the social scope of the hidden transcript.... *It is only when this hidden transcript is openly declared that subordinates can fully recognize the full extent to which their claims, their dreams, their anger is shared by other subordinates with whom they have not been in direct touch.*" Clearly, Scott's

proposition about the relation of small group size and safe expression does not apply to subordinated women within heterosexual couples; his larger point concerning the privatization of the experience of the oppressed is, however, directly relevant to women.

44. There is undoubtedly a tension, if not a flat contradiction, between this classical thesis concerning the critical consciousness of the proletariat and Marx's equally famous dictum that "the ideas of the ruling class are in every epoch the ruling ideas.... The class which has the means of material production at its disposal, has control at the same time over the means of mental production, so that thereby, generally speaking, the ideas of those who lack the means of production are subject to it." *German Ideology*, p. 64. The valid kernels of the two theses can be preserved, and their assertions reconciled, when both are trimmed and nuanced: in capitalist democracies, ideological hegemony (or the ruling ideas) is taken to refer to the framing of mainstream discourse rather than a more literal interpretation of the complete mental subjection of subordinates; secondly, while there is ample evidence of workers' oppositional dispositions, we have also illustrated that this does not readily translate into a full-scale revolutionary (or counter-hegemonic) consciousness due to the material limitations of their position and the nature of their employment dependency.

45. "Let us therefore, in company with the owner of money and the owner of labour-power, leave this noisy sphere where everything takes place on the surface and in full view of everyone, and follow them into the hidden abode of production, on whose threshold there hangs the notice: No admittance except on business." Marx, *Capital* Volume 1, p. 172.

46. This is a persistent theme in the autobiographical writings by male workers extending from the Industrial Revolution to the present. See, for example, Burnett, 1974; Tressell, 1974; Spencer, 1978; Theriault, 1995.

47. We need to appreciate the paradox of being articulate. On the one hand, linguistic competence entails conformity to an assigned vocabulary, to the rules of grammar, to recognized speech patterns and cultural idioms. This is a necessary submission to an externally imposed set of rules; it gives the structure of language its deep and inescapable influence upon thought which has so impressed the postmodernists. But we ought not to ignore the other side of the discursive equation. Linguistic mastery (i.e., extensive conformity) is liberating and empowering. By maximizing her communicative impact upon others, the articulate speaker can wield language in order to develop her distinctive viewpoint, to disseminate it widely and persuasively, to induce others to co-operate with her in common cause.

48. Jameson, for example, claims that the older psychological maladies of alienation and anomie have been replaced by drastic fragmentation, "the 'death' of the subject itself - the end of the autonomous bourgeois monad or ego or individual ... a once-existing centered subject, in th eperiod of classical capitalism and the nuclear family, has today, in the world of organizational bureaucracy, dissolved." (1991, p.15)

49. These arguments are elaborated in Dennis H. Wrong's *The Problem of Order*, Cambridge, Harvard University Press, 1994, pp. 37-109.

50. In many passages, Foucault effectively denies individuals the capacity for self-determing action. "The individual is an effect of power ... an element of its articulation. The individual that power has constituted is at the same time its vehicle" (1908, p.98). As McGowan remarks, Foucault's "view of power offers no way to explain how successful opposition to power could ever occur" (1991, p.126)
51. Cynthia Kaufman and JoAnn Marin, "The Chasm of the Political in Postmodern Theory," *Rethinking Marxism*, Vol.7, # 4, 1994, p. 89.
53. The extensive empirical research on cognitive dissonance initiated by Leon Festinger and his colleagues in the 1950s documented very strong tendencies toward conscious integration of disparate aspects of personal identity as well as the persistence of unresolved contradictions. See Festinger, *Cognitive Dissonance*, San Francisco, W.H. Freeman, 1962. The related research led by Gerhard Lenski in *Power and Privilege* (New York, McGraw Hill, 1966) on tendencies toward status crystallization was indicative of similarly strong integrative tendencies in contending class-related aspects of personal identity. We can find no compelling empirical evidence to indicate that these tendencies have diminished in more recent times.
54. Craig Calhoun, *Nationalism*, University of Minnesota Press, 1997, p. 19.
55. Philosophical doubts concerning the integral self are not new in the history of Western thought, but have been decisively strengthened with the ascendance of post-structuralism. See, for example, John Elster, ed., *The Multiple Self*, Cambridge University Press, 1986. Ours is not a philosophical refutation of the multiple self, based upon a theoretical preference for an integral conception. We are making an empirical claim that most people resist mental fragmentation and strive to integrate their various identities in what *they* regard as a unitary self. We choose to recognize and honour that striving. It is ontologically grounded in the singularity of the individual as an embodied human being, complete with an assigned name and a recognizably unique appearance and identity.
56. Fredric Jameson, *Postmodernism or, the Cultural Logic of Late Capitalism*, Duke University Press, 1994.
57. Appleby, Hunt and Jacob, 1994, p. 202.
58. Broadly sympathetic to the Left, Derrida comments candidly on the dilemma of his apolitical stance. "I try where I can to act politically while recognizing that such action remains incommensurate with my intellectual project of deconstruction." (McGowan, 1991, pp. 110-11).
59. In passionate defence of *différence* against the universalizing pretensions of Western thought, Lyotard condemns any cross-cultural project of scientific generalization, since no common measure exists for the adjudication of language games between different cultures. From this position, he concludes that "reason and power are one and the same thing. You may disguise the one with dialectics or prospectiveness, but you will still have the other in all its crudeness: jails, taboos, public weal, selection, genocide" (1984, p.11). See McGowan's discussion, (1991, pp 180-210).
59. Jameson, whose work we greatly admire, writes glibly of the disappearance

of the individual subject , while claiming that the loss of the concept of self-consciousness (or indeed of consciousness either) [is not] necessarily fatal to the very conception of agency itself (1991, p.16, p. 246). How a notion of purposeful agency could survive the loss of self-consciousness is beyond us.

60. Martin-Barbera's work provides many examples of these interactive mediations of media content, as does the entire corpus of audience receptivity research (*op. cit.*, 1993).

61. Fredric Jameson (1991) holds that in the postmodern era, the media no longer dominate in this way: "If the ideas of the ruling class were once the dominant (or hegemonic) ideology of bourgeois society, the advanced capitalist countries today are now a field of stylistic and discursive heterogeneity without a norm. Faceless masters continue to inflect the economic strategies which constrain our existence, but they no longer need to impose speech (or are henceforth unable to) ..." (p. 17). We cannot square this position with the concerted ideological campaigns of the Right to blame governments for every economic ill and to herald the workings of the free market as benefitting almost everyone once states are prevented from interfering in its affairs. This has been a (largely successful) normative drive to frame a discourse which disarms criticism of capitalism and makes a reasoned discussion of non-market alternatives seem foolish.

62. See the documentation of these trends in Schor (1991). On continuing increases in many of the dimensions of underemployment in the G7 countries and particularly among the working-class and visible minorities, see Livingstone (1999).

63. Greg's reference to "everybody" being called back no longer refers to his thousands of 1984 Stelco brothers and few sisters who are now on permanent layoff, to say nothing of the large numbers of underclass people who have no prospect of decent jobs, partly as a consequence of the same increased overtime by the dwindling core of the fully employed labour force.

64. Marx's description of this process in the *Communist Manifesto* remains relevant: "The bourgeoisie, wherever it has got the upper hand, has put an end to all feudal, patriarchal, idyllic relations. It has piteously torn asunder the motley ties that bound man to his 'natural superiors' and has left remaining no other nexus between man and man than naked self-interest, than callous cash payment. It has drowned the most heavenly ecstasies of religious fervour, of chivalrous enthusiasm, of philistine sentimentalism, in the icy water of egotistical calculation. It has resolved personal worth into exchange value..." (1974a, p. 70).

65. For a fuller account of the "accelerated continuity thesis" with specific attention to the global and Canadian steel industries, as well as a detailed case study of changes at Stelco's Hilton Works in Hamilton, see Corman et. al. (1993).

66. "National sovereignty is eroded from above by the mobility of capital, goods and information across national boundaries, the integration of world capital markets, and the transnational character of industrial production." (Sandel, 1996, p. 74).

67. To cite just one Canadian example, the Solidarity Computer Conferencing Network (SOLINET) is an electronic mail system that is used by union members, the NDP, Action Canada and many other progressive working people. As of the

time of writing, the source for further information was: SOLINET, 21 Florence Street, Ottawa, Ontario K2P 0W6; phone (613) 237-1590; FAX (613) 237-1468. This network was initiated by the Canadian Union of Public Employees.
68. This happened at Stelco's Hilton Works with a wildcat strike in 1966. For an account, see Freeman *op. cit.* One of the most insightful comparative case studies of the explosion of long-simmering worker grievances in large work places during the 1980s is provided by Rick Fantasia (1988). It should also be noted here that more than once, social scientists have confidently claimed that steel or auto workers were overwhelmingly acquiescent and opposed to strikes, only to find workers enthusiastically taking strike actions immediately after the release of such findings. Classic examples are the Lubell poll of U.S. steelworkers in 1959 which was followed by a four month nation strike, and the Goldthorpe study of British Vauxhall's affluent workers in the early 1970s which preceded a wildcat strike of the same plant. We suggest that processes of open struggle by the women's and civil rights movements have had similar dynamics.
69. See *The Mass Psychology of Fascism* (1946) and *Dialectical Materialism and Psychoanalysis* (1947).
70. The most substantial efforts to date in the Canadian case are probably associated with the Canadian Auto Workers' union. See, for example, Gindin (1995).

References

Abercrombie, Nicholas, Stephen Hill, and Bryan Turner. 1980. *The Dominant Ideology Thesis*. London: George Allen and Unwin.

Anderson, Perry. 1998. *The Origins of Postmodernity*. London: Verso.

Appleby, Joyce, Lynn Hunt, and Margaret Jacob. 1994. *Telling the Truth about History*. New York: Norton.

Armstrong, Philip, Andrew Glyn, and John Harrison. 1984. *Capitalism Since 1945*. London: Fontana.

Baudrillard, Jean. 1981. *For a Critique of the Political Economy of the Sign*. St. Louis: Telos Press.

Best, Steven and Douglas Kellner. 1991. *Postmodern Theory: Critical Interrogations.* New York: Guildford Press.

Brennan, Teresa. 1992. *The Interpretation of the Flesh: Freud and Femininity*. London: Routledge.

Burnett, James. 1974. *Useful Toil: Autobiographies of Working People from the 1820s to the 1920s*. London: Allen Lane.

Butler, Judith. 1993. *Bodies That Matter, On the Discursive Limits of "Sex"*. London: Routledge.

Calhoun, Craig. 1995. *Critical Social Theory, Culture, History and the Challenge of Difference*.

Cambridge: Blackwell.

Calhoun, Craig. 1997. *Nationalism*. Minneapolis, University of Minnesota Press.

Callinicos, Alex. 1989. *Against Postmodernism*: A Marxist Critique. New York: St. Martin's Press.

Chomsky, N. and E.S. Herman. 1988. *Manufacturing Consent: The Political Economy of the Mass Media*. New York: Pantheon.

Connell, R.W. 1995. *Masculinities*. Cambridge: Polity Press.

Corman, June, D.W. Livingstone, Meg Luxton, and Wally Seccombe. 1993. *Recasting Steel Labour: The Stelco Story*. Halifax, N.S.: Fernwood Publications.

Derrida, Jacques. 1978. *Writing and Difference*. Chicago: University of Chicago Press.

Dews, Peter. 1987. *Logics of Disintegration*. London: Verso.

Eagleton, Terry. 1996. *The Illusions of Postmodernism*. Cambridge Mass.: Blackwell.

Eagleton, Terry. 1991. *Ideology, An Introduction*. London: Verso.

Ehrenreich, Barbara. 1989. *Fear of Falling: The Inner Life of the Middle Class*. New York: Pantheon.

Elster, John, ed. 1986. *The Multiple Self*. Cambridge: Cambridge University Press.

Fantasia, Rick. 1988. *Cultures of Solidarity: Consciousness, Action and Contemporary American Workers*. Berkeley: University of California Press.

Festinger, Leon. 1962. *Cognitive Dissonance*. San Francisco: W.H. Freeman.

Foucault, Michel. 1977. *Discipline and Punish: The Birth of the Prison*. London: Allen Lane/Penguin.

Foucault, Michel. 1980. *Power/Knowledge: Selected Interviews and Other Writings 1972-1977*. New York: Pantheon.

Fraser, Nancy. 1997. *Justice Interruptus, Critical Reflections on the "Post-socialist" Condition*.

London: Routledge.

Freeman, Bill. 1982. *1005: Political Life in a Union Local*. Toronto: Lorimer.

Freeman, Richard B. and Rogers, Joel. 1999. *What Workers Want*. Ithaca, Cornell University Press.

Freud, Sigmund. 1923. *The Ego and the Id*. London: Hogarth Press.

Freud, Sigmund. 1930. *Civilization and Its Discontents*. New York: Cape & Smith.

Freud, Sigmund. 1955 [1920]. *Beyond the Pleasure Principle*. London: Hogarth Press.

Genovese, Eugene. 1972. *Roll, Jordan, Roll: The World the Slaves Made*. New York: Random House.

Geras, Norman. 1988. "Ex-Marxism without Substance: Being a Real Reply to Laclau and Mouffe." *New Left Review*, 169.

Gindin, Sam. 1995. *The Canadian Auto Workers: The Birth and Transformation of a Union*. Toronto: Lorimer.

Goldthorpe, John. 1983. "Women and Class Analysis: In Defence of the Conventional View." *Sociology*, 17,4.

Goldthorpe, John. 1984. "Women and Class Analysis: A Reply to the Replies." *Sociology*, 18,4.

Goldthorpe, John, C. Llewellyn, and C. Payne. 1980. *Social Mobility and Class Structure in Modern Britain*. Oxford: Clarendon Press.

Goldthorpe, John and Gordon Marshall. 1992. "The Promising Future of Class Analysis: A Response to Recent Critiques." *Sociology*, 26,3.

Goldthorpe, John and C. Payne. 1986. "On the Class Mobility of Women: Results from Different Approaches to the Analysis of Recent British Data." *Sociology*, 20.

Hall, Stuart. "The Question of Cultural Identity". In Stuart Hall, David Held, Don Hubert & Kenneth Thompson, eds. *Modernity, An Introduction to Modern Societies*. Cambridge: Blackwell.

Hanagan, Michael P., Leslie Page Moch and Wayne Te Brake. 1998. *Challenging Authority, the Historical Study of Contentious Politics*. Minneapolis, University of Minnesota Press.

Harvey, David. 1990. *The Condition of Post-Modernism*. Oxford: Basil Blackwell.

Hewitt, Patricia. 1993. *About Time, The Revolution in Work and Family Life*. London: Rivers Oram Press.

Hill, Stuart, Donald Rothchild and Colin Cameron. 1998. "Tactical Information and the Diffusion of Peaceful Protests." In *The International Spread of Ethnic Conflict, Fear, Diffusion and Escalation*. Princeton, N.J., Princeton University Press.

Hobson, Dorothy. 1996. "Housewives and the Mass Media." In Paul Marris and Sue Thornham, editors, *Media Studies, A Reader*. Edinburgh: Edinburgh University Press.

Honneth, Axel. 1996. *The Struggle for Recognition, the Moral Grammar of Social Conflicts.*
Cambridge, Mass. MIT Press.
Ignatieff, Michael. 1998. *The Warrior"s Honour.* Toronto: Penguin.
Innis, Harold. 1950. *Empire and Communications.* Oxford: Clarendon Press.
Innis, Harold. 1951. *The Bias of Communication.* Toronto: University of Toronto Press.
Jameson, Fredric. 1972. *Prison-House of Language.* Princeton: Princeton University Press.
Jameson, Fredric. 1991. *Postmodernism, or, the Cultural Logic of Late Capitalism.* Durham, N.C.: Duke University Press.
Kaufman, Cynthia and JoAnn Marin. 1994. "The Chasm of the Political in Postmodern Theory." *Rethinking Marxism,* 7,4.
Laclau, Ernesto and Chantal Mouffe. 1985. *Hegemony and Socialist Strategy.* London: Verso.
Leitch, Vincent B. 1996. *Postmodernism, Local Effects, Global Flows.* New York: State University of New York Press.
Lenin, V.I. 1970. *Selected Works, Volume 1.* Moscow, Progress Publishers.
Lenski, Gerhard. 1966. *Power and Privilege.* New York: McGraw-Hill.
Leys, Colin. 1999. "The Public Sphere and the Media: Market Supremacy Versus Democracy."
In *Socialist Register.* London: Merlin Press.
Livingstone, David W. 1983. *Class, Ideologies and Educational Futures.* London and New York: Falmer Press.
Livingstone, David W. 1987. "Class Position, Class Consciousness and Political Preference in Hard Times." In *Working People in Hard Times: Canadian Perspectives,* ed. R. Argue, C. Gannage, and D.W. Livingstone. Toronto: Garamond Press.
Livingstone, David W. 1999. *The Education-Jobs Gap: Underemployment or Economic Democracy.* Boulder, Col.: Westview Press and Toronto: Garamond Press.
Livingstone, David W. 1999. *Public Attitudes Toward Education in Ontario 1998: The Twelfth OISE/UT Survey.* Toronto: University of Toronto Press.
Livingstone, D.W. and Meg Luxton. 1996. "Gender Consciousness at Work: Modifications of the Male Breadwinner Norm." In David Livingstone and J. Marshall Mangan, editors, *Recast Dreams: Class and Gender Consciousness in Steeltown.* Toronto: Garamond Press.
Livingstone, David and J. Marshall Mangan, editors.1996. *Recast Dreams: Class and Gender Consciousness in Steeltown.* Toronto: Garamond Press.
Livingstone, D.W. and Reuben Roth. 1998. "Workplace Communities and Transformative Learning: Oshawa Autoworkers and the CAW", Convergence, Vol. 31, # 3, pp. 12-23.
Luxton, Meg and June Corman, 2000 (forthcoming). *Getting by in Hard Times: Gender and Class Relations in Steeltown,* Toronto: University of Toronto Press.

Lyotard, Jean-Francois. 1984a. *The Postmodern Condition*. Minneapolis: University of Minnesota Press.

Lyotard, Jean-Francois. 1984b. *Driftworks*. New York: Semiotext(e).

Macpherson, C.B. 1962. *The Political Theory of Possessive Individualism*. Oxford: Oxford University Press.

Maddison, Angus. 1982. *Phases of Capitalist Development*. Oxford: Oxford University Press.

Mann, Michael. 1970. "The Social Cohesion of Liberal Democracy." *American Sociological Review*, 35,3.

Mann, Michael. 1973. *Consciousness and Action among the Western Working Class*. London: Macmillan.

Mann, Michael. 1995. "Sources of Variation in Working Class Movements in Twentieth Century Europe." *New Left Review*, 212.

Marris, Paul and Sue Thornham, editors. 1996. *Media Studies, A Reader*. Edinburgh: Edinburgh University Press.

Martin-Barbera, Jesus. 1993. *Communication, Culture and Hegemony: From the Media to Mediations*. London: Sage.

Marx, Karl. 1963. *Selected Writings in Sociology and Social Philosophy*. Harmondsworth, England: Penguin.

Marx, Karl. 1967 [1867]. *Capital, Volume 1*. New York: International Publishers.

Marx, Karl. 1974a. "Manifesto of the Communist Party." In *Karl Marx, Political Writings Volume 1*. New York: Vintage Books.

Marx, Karl. 1974b. *Surveys from Exile: Political Writings*. New York: Vintage Books.

Marx, Karl. 1977. *Selected Writings*. Oxford: Oxford University Press.

Marx, Karl and Frederick Engels. 1970 [1846]. *The German Ideology*. Part I. Ed. C.J. Arthur. New York: International Publications.

McGowan, John. 1991. *Postmodernism and Its Critics*. Ithaca, Cornell University Press.

Meiksins, Peter. 1987a. "New Classes and Old Theories: The Impasse of Contemporary Class Analysis." In *Recapturing Marxism: An Appraisal of Recent Trends in Sociological Theory*, ed. R. Levine and J. Lembeke. New York: Praeger.

Meiksins, Peter. 1987b. "White Collar Workers and the Process of Class Formation." In *Working People and Hard Times*, ed. R. Argue, C. Gannage, and David W. Livingstone. Toronto: Garamond Press.

Meszaros, I. 1970. "Contingent and Necessary Class Consciousness." In *Aspects of History and Class Consciousness*, ed. I. Meszaros. London: Routledge and Kegan Paul.

Morely, David. 1996. "Cultural Transformations: the Politics of Resistance." In Paul Marris and Sue Thornham, editors, *Media Studies, A Reader*. Edinburgh: Edinburgh University Press.

Newman, Katherine S. 1988. *Falling from Grace: The Experience of Downward Mobility in the American Middle Class*. New York: Free Press.

Piaget, Jean. 1954. *The Construction of Reality in the Child*. New York: Basic Books.

Reich, Wilhelm. 1946. *The Mass Psychology of Fascism*. New York: Orgone Institute Press.

Reich, Wilhelm. 1947. *Dialectical Materialism and Psychoanalysis*. New York: Orgone Institute Press.

Rosenau, Pauline M. 1992. *Post-Modernism and the Social Sciences*. Princeton: Princeton University Press.

Rubin, Lillian. 1976. *Worlds of Pain: Life in the Working-Class Family*. New York: Basic Books.

Rubin, Lillian. 1983. *Intimate Strangers: Men and Women Together*. New York: Harper and Row.

Rubin, Lillian. 1994. *Families on the Faultline: America"s Working Class Speaks about the Family, the Economy, Race, and Ethnicity*. New York: Harper Collins.

Ryan, Michael. 1982. *Marxism and Deconstruction*. Baltimore: John Hopkins University Press.

Schor, Juliet. 1991. *The Overworked American*. New York: Basic Books.

Scott, James C. 1990. *Domination and the Arts of Resistance: Hidden Transcripts*. New Haven, Conn.: Yale University Press.

Seccombe, Wally. 1992. *A Millennium of Family Change, Feudalism to Capitalism in Northwestern Europe*. London: Verso.

Seccombe, Wally. 1993. *Weathering the Storm: Working-Class Families from the Industrial Revolution to the Fertility Decline*. London: Verso.

Seccombe, Wally. 1999. "Contradictions of Shareholder Capitalism: Downsizing Jobs, Enlisting Savings, Destabilizing Families" in *Socialist Register*. London: Merlin Press.

Spencer, Charles. 1978. *Blue Collar: An Internal Examination of the Workplace*. Chicago: Vanguard Books.

Theriault, Reg. 1995. *How to Tell When You"re Tired: A Brief Examination of Work*. New York: Norton.

Tressell, Robert. 1974. *The Ragged-Trousered Philanthropist*. New York: Monthly Review Press.

Vygotsky, L. 1978. *Mind in Society*. Cambridge, Mass.: Harvard University Press.

Wallerstein, Emmanuel. 1979. *The Capitalist World-Economy*. Cambridge: Cambridge University Press.

Wilson, E.C. 1993. *The Ghetto Underclass: Social Science Perspectives*. Newbury Park, Cal.: Sage.

Wilson, W. 1987. *The Truly Disadvantaged: The Inner City, the Underclass, and Public Policy*. Chicago: University of Chicago Press.

Wrong, Dennis H. 1994. *The Problem of Order*. Cambridge: Harvard University Press.

Index

AGMV
MARQUIS
Québec, Canada
1999